THE STAR WARS

CRAFT BOOK

THE STAR WARS CRAFT BOOK

Bonnie Burton

TITAN BOOKS
LONDON

Lucasfilm
Executive editor: J. W. Rinzler
Art director: Troy Alders
Director of publishing: Carol Roeder

Published in the UK, Ireland and Australia by Titan Books, a division of Titan Publishing Group Ltd, 144 Southwark Street, London SE1 0UP.
A CIP catalogue record for this title is available from the British Library.
ISBN 9780857686176
Printed in the United States
www.starwars.com
www.titanbooks.com
2 4 6 8 9 7 5 3 1
First Edition
Interior design by Foltz Design

Photos on pages 9, 11, and 84 by Mark Maguire
Photos on pages 19, 43, 85, 106, 107, 121, 123, and 156 by Bradford Foltz
Photo on page 42 by GK Hart/Vikki Hart/The Image Bank/Getty Images
Photos on page 41 courtesy of Sammi Resendes
Photo on page 81 courtesy of Kayla Kromer
Crocheted General Grievous photo on page 102 courtesy of Amber Mendenhall
All other photos by Robert Sondgroth, photographed at Sintak Studios, San Francisco, CA, 2010

Dedicated to Geeky Craftsters everywhere. May the glue gun be with you!

ACKNOWLEDGMENTS

This craftastic book would not have been possible without a big list of fantastic people who love glitter glue as much as I do! A huge thanks must first go out to the Jedi Master of patience and wisdom, my Random House book editor, Erich Schoeneweiss. He kept me focused and on task—which is no easy feat. If there's a craft-book-editing pageant, Erich wins the crown! Thanks a zillion times to Nancy Delia, April Flores, David Stevenson, and the rest of the Random House team who had fun with the craft projects, made the photos look snazzier, and created a cover worthy of a Sith Lord. And thanks to Brad Foltz for his beautiful book design.

Big thanks go to Carol Roeder, Jonathan Rinzler, Troy Alders, and the rest of Lucas Books who championed this project from the get-go and let me unleash my crafting addiction to the masses.

A special shout-out goes to my Lucas Online family at Lucasfilm—most importantly my Online editorial manager Pablo Hidalgo, for letting me start a craft section on Starwars.com just for kids. Thanks to my awesome co-workers Matt Martin, Jon Freel, Nicole Love, Pete Vilmur, Sean Haeberman, Steve Sansweet, Mary Franklin, Tracy Cannobbio, and others who encouraged my crafting addiction with ideas, coffee, and pats on the back. Thanks also to my Lucas Online boss, Bill Gannon, for allowing me to expense googly eyes and pipe cleaners.

Model and craft sidekick Amanda Jean Camarillo deserves endless candy for helping me show off the crafts in the book.

Thanks to photographer Bob Sondgroth for making my crafts look like supermodels.

Thanks to my craft stunt double Terri Hodges, who helped sew, glue, and glitter last-minute projects and can often be seen next to me at conventions making Ewok sock puppets. Thanks to artists Tom Hodges, Cat Staggs, and Dennis Von-Galle for designing patterns for this book.

Thanks to Craftzine.com, io9.com, BoingBoing.net and Geek Dad for blogging about my craft projects over the years, as well as *Make* magazine, who invited me to teach the next DIY generation to make *Star Wars* crafts at their annual Bay Area Maker Faire.

Thanks to the San Francisco toy store Great Stuff for always having the craft supplies I need to finish projects at the eleventh hour. I love any store that has marble animal eyes, plastic insects, and tasty treats—all under one roof.

Thanks to my parents, who encouraged me to make dolls, puppets, and art by giving me a craft room. My mom always says, "Only boring people get bored." Because of that mantra, I've never run out of crafty ways to celebrate my love for *Star Wars*.

Lastly, thanks to the Maker—George Lucas—for creating a galaxy full of muses who have never failed to inspire, entertain, and keep me daydreaming ever since I was a youngling.

CONTENTS

INTRODUCTION

THESE ARE THE CRAFTS YOU'RE LOOKING FOR . . .

There's nothing more fun than transforming a boring old washcloth into a cuddly wampa, or a piece of felt into a whimsical Yoda puppet. Ever since I was a kid, I've devoted hours to making crafts out of everything from empty paper towel rolls to tattered pillowcases. I've most likely been covered in a thin layer of craft glitter since the age of seven. Even though I'm all grown up, I still can't help but put googly eyes on everything in sight.

Crafts aren't just a solo hobby. Creative folks like to hang out with one another, and this book is chock-full of crafts that can be shared with family and friends. Make a bunch of cantina puppets and put on a show. Ask your friends to come over and bring extra-extra-large *Star Wars* shirts to transform into pillows, bags, and quilts. Make dioramas and take photos of your action figures having the time of their tiny lives.

NO FORCE-SENSITIVE SKILLS REQUIRED

All the crafts in this book are meant to be easy enough for kids and adults alike. Crafts are meant to be fun, not frustrating. While some of the projects may take a couple of days to complete, most of them can be finished in an afternoon. There's no need to know fancy sewing stitches. Basic sewing skills are just fine here. You don't even need a sewing machine!

While this book won't show you how to make a working protocol droid, you will learn how to make *Star Wars* art, puppets, dolls, jewelry, and more. Many of these crafts use cheap materials, items found around the house and even in your recycling bin.

One of this book's goals is to inspire you to see craft projects in items most people would throw away. A holey sock gets a new life as a puppet. Shrunken sweaters become toys. Strips of newspaper become a Geonosian arena creature. An extra-large shirt at the bottom of your closet can finally be useful as a tote bag. Once you know how to turn something ordinary into something extraordinary, inspiration will follow you everywhere.

HOW TO USE THIS BOOK

Directions are easy to read and the crafts are divided into sections: Playtime, Home Décor, Holiday Crafts, Nature & Science Crafts, and *Star Wars* Style. Most supplies in this book can be found in any craft store or around your house. There are handy tips throughout on how to get the most out of your crafting, as well as interviews with other fans who have made everything from *Star Wars* costumes to a light-up *Millennium Falcon* bed.

THE POINT IS TO HAVE FUN!

The following are materials you should always have on hand for crafting at a moment's notice. While some of the items listed are available at craft stores, you can also find a wealth of materials at thrift stores, dollar stores, and even your own recycling bin. Begin training yourself to look at trash as possible treasure and you'll never run out of possible crafting ideas. Organize materials in shoe boxes, envelopes, jars, or whatever you have handy with a lid.

Basic Supplies

Bags: You know that big bag of paper and plastic grocery bags you keep planning to recycle? You can use those in your crafts! Use small brown paper bags for puppets. Plastic bags make excellent stuffing material.

Binder clips: These work great to keep things in place while you're gluing something together.

Buttons: Use for closures or cutesy eyes. Store in a jar for easy access.

Chalk wheel/pencil: This is a handy tool for tracing out patterns onto fabric. It's also great for freehand drawing onto fabrics because it will wash off without leaving a mark.

Colored pens, pencils, and crayons: Great for drawing crafts as well as mail art.

Craft kits: No one says you have to start from scratch. You can sometimes save time and money with all-in-one craft kits for jewelry, bird houses, rugs, pillows, tree ornaments, quilts, dolls, mosaics, and more. Stock up on these kits when you see them on sale, and then customize one for a project you'd like to tackle.

Dried pasta/beans/rice: Sometimes playing with your food is encouraged! Dried pasta and beans can make interesting crafting supplies when you're creating textured art portraits. Choose beans with colors that suit your needs, or just paste the dried food onto a canvas and paint over it.

Fabric: Keep basic colors of fabric on hand in a big bin. Always keep in mind how you can reuse old clothes, blankets, bedding, and socks for a craft before you throw anything away.

Felt: You can find felt by the ream or in squares in every color in the rainbow. The best way to build up your collection is by getting assorted color packs of felt. Oftentimes this is the cheapest route as well. Felt also comes in stiffer styles, as well as in metallic and glitter. So feel free to mix and match styles to make more interesting dolls, puppets, and other felt crafts. Don't forget to save the scraps to use as stuffing.

Glitter: This crafting embellishment can be addicting. It adds a bit of sparkle and glamour to every project. But be aware that no matter how much newspaper you put down or vacuuming you do afterward, glitter gets everywhere and never goes away. Think of glitter as the Force—it's everywhere around you!

Googly eyes: This is the one craft supply you'll never get tired of. Googly eyes give your dolls and puppets personality! They come in all shapes, colors, and sizes—including some with painted-on eyelashes! Glue them right onto your creation, or get even easier-to-apply self-adhesive eyes. Personally, I like to glue them onto my food containers, so I can pretend my food has parties in my fridge when I'm not there.

Glue: Every crafter has his or her favorite brand of glue. Try out different brands of fabric, wood, glass, glitter, spray-on, and simple craft glue to see what works best for you and the project at hand. Specialty glue can get on the pricey side. Make sure to have a supply of basic craft glue as a backup. For the felt crafts, use a strong (fast-drying) fabric glue. Try using spray-on adhesive for paper crafts as a quick-drying glue option as well.

Jewelry supplies: Depending on your skill set, you can make brooches, necklaces, bracelets, and rings from scratch using specialty backings and supplies. Most craft stores have individual jewelry elements, or you can buy kits. If you want to skip all that and just découpage or refashion existing jewelry, that's the quickest route to creating fun *Star Wars* bling.

Needle-nose plier: This is an ideal tool for jewelry making as well as other projects that may involve wire.

Paints: Acrylics, watercolors, poster paint, and any medium you prefer to use in your crafts. Experiment with different kinds of paints (glitter, oil, latex, and so on) to get the effects you want—whether it's glossy or matte.

Paintbrushes: Get a selection of good-quality natural and synthetic brushes for painting, gluing, découpaging, and more. Just remember to clean them with mild soap and water after every use to keep them in long-lasting shape.

Plasticine clay: The two brands most often used are Sculpey and Fimo. These crafting clays are ideal for sculpting everything from doll heads to creature teeth. This malleable clay comes in a variety of colors and bakes hard in a regular oven.

Pipe cleaners (also called chenille stems): Get them in every color! Great for making puppet and doll limbs bendy.

Sandpaper: Keep a stack of sheets on hand in case you need to sand down rough edges on your wood or metal crafts. This also can be used to give a surface more texture before you découpage a project.

Sealant: Many art sealants come in spray-on form and are ideal for making your final piece of art more permanent. Make sure you spray in a well-ventilated area.

Scissors: Don't go to crazy in the craft store when buying scissors. (They can get pricey!) Try on a few pairs to see how they fit in your hands. Many even have padded handles, which are more comfortable for your hands, especially if you plan on cutting a lot of fabric. Get a couple of basic pairs of cheap craft scissors for cutting paper. Pinking shears are great to give fabrics a decorative edge while preventing threads from unraveling. Smaller scissors are best for delicate découpage paper crafts. *Tip:* Make sure you tie a piece of yarn around the handle of your fabric scissors so you always know which pair are for cutting fabric and which are for basic paper crafts. That way you don't dull your fabric scissors. Remember to get pairs sharpened at a hardware store periodically to keep them in tip-top crafting shape.

Sewing stuff: Sewing needles, a pincushion, a seam ripper, straight pins, and safety pins are ideal

to have on hand for any sewing project. You can buy all of these items separately, or get everything at once in a handy sewing kit.

Tape measure and ruler: These come in handy when you need to measure out fabrics, paper, wood, and other crafting materials. Plus, rulers are great for making a straight edge.

Tape: Masking, clear, duct, and packing tape should be in your craft arsenal at all times. Use tape for papier-mâché projects, mail art, and even a cheap version of lamination.

Thread: A basic cotton/poly-blend thread is ideal for most projects. Get the colors you need just for a specific project, as well as regularly used colors such as black and white. You don't always have to match the thread color to the fabric color. Get creative by mixing colors to create a unique look to your stitch work. Embroidery thread is ideal for cross-stitch projects and makes a thicker decorative thread for pillows, dolls, and T-shirt embellishments.

X-Acto knife/razors: When you need more precision than a pair of scissors, use an X-Acto or razor. Just be careful!

Yarn: While it's tempting to buy every color of yarn in the craft store, you don't need to stock up on tons of it right away. Only get the colors you need, and try to hit stores during special yarn sales. Depending on your project, you might only need basic cotton/poly-blend yarn, but feel free to experiment with different materials such as wool and bamboo blends.

Odds and Ends

Bottles and jars: Whether it's plastic or glass, you can use these as storage containers, paintbrush holders, flower vases, candleholders, plant terrariums, and even doll bodies.

Broken action figures: Don't throw those out! They can be given a second life as jewelry, cuff links, magnets, hair accessories, and even wreaths! Store them in a plastic bin so you can use parts as needed.

Chopsticks: If you get a lot of Chinese takeout, you probably have a small pile of wooden chopsticks. These work great as a tool to get stuffing into hard-to-reach places such as doll arms. Or use them for stick puppets!

Comics: If you have extra *Star Wars* comics that you're not intending to read again, you can tear out pages to make interesting découpage elements for crafts. If you prefer to keep your comics intact, color-copy them or scan and print out pages to use instead.

Frames: These can get pricey brand-new, so visit a thrift store for cheap art sold in cool frames. While the artworks might be discards, you can find interesting and useful frames to showcase your own art.

Games: Instead of trashing old board games, trading cards, chess pieces, word tiles, dice, and other gaming accessories, use them in your crafts. It's even better if they happen to be from *Star Wars* games. Give that *Millennium Falcon* game piece another life as a clever necklace pendant!

Laminating machine: Because many of these basic machines are so cheap (usually under thirty dollars), it's a good investment to make if you plan on crafting items such as place mats, durable art, flash cards, playing cards, greeting cards, name tags, luggage tags, and jewelry.

Linens: Old hankies, washcloths, towels, bedding, tablecloths, and dish towels are great materials for *Star Wars* embroidery projects, dolls, pillows, and samplers. Don't stick with just white. Exciting prints and bold colors can also work as fun crafting backdrops. Think of it as a very soft piece of canvas to display your art!

Magazines: Great for cutting up images and letters for mail art and découpage projects.

Masks: Keep those old Halloween masks! You can always transform animal masks into papier-mâché *Star Wars* creatures.

Newspapers: These are the ultimate cheap crafting material when it comes to a papier-mâché project. Newspapers can be wadded up or cut into wide strips to use in your sculpting projects. They also are great to cover tables for especially messy crafts.

Notebooks: Even a boring notebook can be transformed by pasting *Star Wars* images to its cover. By decorating blank notebooks with your favorite characters and scenes, you've already upgraded something mundane into a cool book to jot down your thoughts, stories, and ideas.

Shoe boxes and cardboard boxes: Before you break down a box for recycling, think about what kind of new life you could give it as a toy diorama, a dollhouse, a puppet stage, or even a craft supplies storage box.

T-shirts: Even if a *Star Wars* T-shirt is too small, too big, or too worn out, you can still make a fun craft from it. Keep old and unused shirts in your supply stash to make pillows, quilts, or even cooler T-shirts.

THE STAR WARS® CRAFT BOOK

PLAYTIME

Making dolls, puppets, toys, and backdrops is a fun way to unleash your creativity while making a creature all your own. *Star Wars* has a rich history in puppets and model making. Yoda started as a puppet, after all! As you make these crafts, think about how you can use them to act out your own plays or puppet shows. Make models and backdrops for your toys as though you're building a set at Industrial Light & Magic.

CHEWBACCA SOCK PUPPET

Everyone needs a loyal co-pilot, and it's easy to make your own Wookiee sidekick with a single sock and a few craft supplies. As you make Chewbacca, keep in mind that you can alter the puppet slightly to create an Ewok or wampa depending on the color of the fur and felt details.

WHAT YOU NEED

- Fake fur
- Old brown or dark color sock
- Scissors
- Needle and thread
- Button
- Chenille stems/pipe cleaners
- Googly eyes
- Brown and grey felt

How to Make a Chewbacca Sock Puppet

1 Fold the fake fur over the heel and toe of the sock so that the edges of the fur align with the edges of the top of the sock. Sew into place, but don't sew the sock closed. ▶

2 Put your hand inside the sock so that your fingers are in the toe area and your thumb is in the heel—making this the mouth area. Glue the eyes in place. Sew the button nose down, but be careful not to sew the sock shut—you should still be able to place your fingers inside.

3 To make the arms, cut two strips of fake fur. Roll each strip around a few chenille stems, and sew the edges and ends together. Sew the arms to the sides of the puppet.

4 Last, cut out a long rectangle strip of brown felt, and sew the ends together to make Chewie's bandolier. Cut out seven small rectangles of gray felt and glue to the bandolier. Cut a thin strip of brown felt and glue it to the middle of the bandolier. Place over Chewie's head so it sits on his body like a sash. ◄

CHEWBACCA
SOCK PUPPET

CANTINA CHARACTERS FINGER PUPPETS

When Luke Skywalker first walked into the Mos Eisley cantina with Ben Kenobi, he saw many unusual and shifty-looking characters lurking around the place. Of course, these make perfect subjects for finger puppets. Grab your favorite *Star Wars* Visual Dictionary or Essential Guide, or go to starwars.com and look up your favorite Cantina patron to re-create in puppet form.

WHAT YOU NEED

- Basic finger puppet pattern (see Appendix)
- Pen and paper
- Scissors
- Fake fur in white, brown, and beige
- Chenille stems/pipe cleaners
- Colored felt squares (brown, beige, black, red, green, gray, tan, orange, white)
- Sewing needle
- Brown, black, gray, white thread
- Straight pins
- Pillow stuffing
- Glue
- Small googly eyes
- Brown and black yarn
- Black beads
- *Star Wars* books and magazines for reference

How to Make Cantina Finger Puppets

1. Trace the basic finger puppet pattern found in the Appendix of this book using scrap paper and a dark pen. Cut out the pattern and set aside. You'll be using this pattern for the basic body to all your puppets.

2 Cut out bodies from the tan, green, and white felt for your finger puppets. Sew the bodies together so that you have basic finger puppet bodies to work with

GREEDO'S
BODY

BITH'S
BODY

MUFTAK'S
BODY

3 Stick pipe cleaners inside the puppet arms to make them bendy. Cut out hands from the scrap felt and sew onto the ends of the arms. You can stitch the fingers for more detail.

4 If you making a furry character, such as Muftak, cut the fake fur to cover the basic body pattern you have sewn. Cover the body, front and back, with the fake fur and glue it to the basic body. You can sew the sides for extra durability. Now cut out more fur to cover the head, allowing it to overlap the body fur a little bit to add some extra dimension. Glue the fur to the basic body's head and sew the sides if you wish.

5 You'll be using felt for the head of your puppet. Be sure to match up the color of the felt with the skin color of your alien. Greedo is green and Bith are off-white. Now look at the head shape of the Cantina alien you wish to make. Bith band members have oval heads. Greedo's head almost looks like the letter Q! Cut out these shapes from various colored pieces of felt depending on their skin color. Match them up with the basic bodies you've already sewn together. Glue the head shapes to the front and back of the puppets to give them more of a 3-D look. Sew the sides if you wish. Add stuffing to the head of the basic body as well.

6 Look closely at the costumes each of the Cantina characters is wearing. Cut out fronts and backs of the clothes you wish to place on your puppets from the felt. Make basic T-shirt, robe, and jacket shapes. You can either glue or sew the costumes on the fronts and

7

craft continues on the next page

8 Once you have everything glued down, you can act out your own favorite moments from the Cantina.

MUFTAK

backs of your puppets. Always be sure not to sew your puppet shut; you want to still be able to get your finger in the opening.

7 Time to give your puppets faces. This is where you give your puppets their expressions and other details that bring them to life. Glue on googly eyes and tiny felt triangles for mouths. Other puppets will require more specific details. Make Bith eyes from medium-sized black felt circles. Cut out a small square, fold it in half, and attach to Greedo's face for his nose. His antennae can be made by making two small cones from felt, and his ears are simply cut from felt and attached. Use black beads for Greedo's eyes! Glue four googly eyes to Muftak's head and give him a long white felt nose.

DESIGN TIP

Lightsabers: To make a lightsaber start by cutting the blade from blue, green, red, yellow, or purple pipe cleaners. For the hilt, roll and glue together a strip of grey, black, or brown felt at the end of the pipe cleaner. Glue onto the puppet's hand or use nylon adhesive tabs such as Velcro.

CANTINA CHARACTER FINGER PUPPETS

BITH
MUSICIAN

GREEDO

YOU CAN CREATE A WHOLE CAST OF *STAR WARS* CHARACTERS TO ADD TO YOUR FINGER PUPPET COLLECTION

Holiday Visitors: Invite your finger puppets to help decorate during your holiday seasons.

GENERAL GRIEVOUS FINGER PUPPET

Act out your favorite scenes from *Revenge of the Sith* and episodes of *Star Wars: The Clone Wars* with this extra-creepy yet cute General Grievous finger puppet!

WHAT YOU NEED

- General Grievous body, head, and arm patterns (see Appendix)
- Scissors
- Light beige, light gray, black, brown, and red felt squares
- Straight pins
- Sewing needle
- Off-white thread
- Glue
- Pipe cleaners/chenille stems—white, green, red, and blue
- Googly eyes
- Self-adhesive nylon fastening tape such as Velcro (optional)

How to Make a General Grievous Finger Puppet

1 Copy and cut out the General Grievous body, head, and arm patterns in the Appendix. Secure the body pattern to two pieces of light beige felt with straight pins. Then cut the felt.

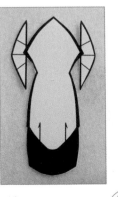

2 Sew the two body pieces of felt together, but don't sew the bottom—that's where your finger will go for the puppeting action. Glue the side head parts to each other instead of sewing them to save time.

3 Cut out thick gray strips of felt. Glue them to Grievous's body to look like his rib cage.

4 Next, use the head pattern so you can cut out a head and glue it on top of your puppet. Glue only the top half of the head to the sewn puppet base so it will have more of a 3-D look to it. ▶

5 Cut out the arm pattern and use it to cut four pairs of arms from the beige felt. Cut small strips of the white pipe cleaner and glue them inside each arm. Wrap and glue gray bands of felt around the elbow and wrist areas of the arms.

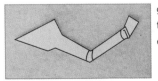

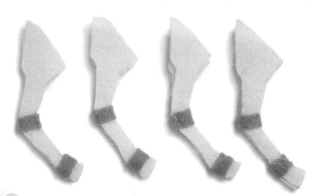

represent his ultrasonic vocabulator. Feel free to add more details from his mask if you would like it to look more authentic.

8. It wouldn't be General Grievous if he didn't have a stolen lightsaber in each hand. Make a lightsaber blade by cutting smaller pieces of red, blue or green pipe cleaners. For the lightsaber hilt, roll and glue together a strip of gray, black, or brown felt at the end of the pipe cleaner. Glue a lightsaber to each hand or...

6. Position the arms and secure them with straight pins to the back of Grievous's body. Sew them to the back, but be careful not to sew your puppet shut.

7. Cut out small red squares of felt and glue them to your puppet's head, then glue the googly eyes on top. This makes him look extra-creepy and evil. Glue gray half circles to his mask, as well as three thin gray strips to

9. If you would like to change around lightsabers when you play with the puppet, you can put small pieces of self-sticking nylon fastening tape such as Velcro on the side of the lightsaber hilt and on his hands. Your puppet is now complete, but you'll have to add the sinister cough.

GENERAL
GRIEVOUS
FINGER
PUPPET

YODA FINGER PUPPET

Judge a puppet by its size, will you? Make up your own stories about the Jedi Master's adventures with this fun Yoda puppet. It's up to you which version you want to make—Prequel Trilogy Yoda, *Clone Wars* Yoda, or Original Trilogy Yoda.

WHAT YOU NEED

- Yoda body, robe front, and robe back patterns (see Appendix)
- Scissors
- Green, brown, red, and gray felt squares
- Straight pins
- Sewing needle

- Brown and green thread
- Chopstick
- Pillow stuffing
- Pipe cleaner/chenille stem
- Glue
- Googly eyes

How to Make a Yoda Finger Puppet

1 Copy and cut out the Yoda body and robe patterns. Secure the Yoda body pattern to two pieces of green felt,

and the front and back robe patterns to the brown felt with straight pins. Then cut the felt.

2 Sew the two pieces of green felt together, but don't sew the bottom—that's where your finger will go for the puppeting action. Use a chopstick to push the pillow stuffing into the head and top half of the body. Cut two small pieces of a pipe cleaner and stick each piece into the arms to make them bendy.

DESIGN TIP

Stick Puppet: For young crafters, instead of sewing, you can glue all the finger puppet pieces of Yoda to a wooden craft stick or chopstick to make a fun and easy stick puppet.

3 Next, sew the robe onto Yoda's body but don't sew the bottom. Don't forget to put the small gray felt square inside the robe.

FRONT

BACK

4 Glue on a small green square for the nose, a small red triangle for the mouth, and googly eyes!

YODA FINGER
PUPPET

15

ADMIRAL SACKBAR PUPPET

It's not a trap! In fact, you'll be recycling while making a cool puppet! Transform boring paper bags into a sassy puppet of Mon Calamari military hero Admiral Ackbar.

WHAT YOU NEED

- 2 small brown paper bags
- Craft glue
- Large googly eyes (optional)

- Black, white, yellow, and beige felt squares
- Scissors

How to Make an Admiral Sackbar Puppet

1 Lay one of the paper bags down with the folded end of the bag faceup on your work surface. Cut the bottom half of other brown bag off and tape to the bottom of the bag to make an extra long bag puppet head. Be sure to crumple up the other bag scraps and stuff into the elongated head to give it some shape.

2 Glue the large googly eyes on the far sides of the head. Or cut out two medium-sized beige felt circles, then two slightly smaller yellow felt circles, and even smaller black felt circles. Glue the black circles onto the yellow circles, and then onto the brown circles to make a pair of eyes. Glue on either side of the bag head.

3 Cut two small black ovals and glue them right above the bag fold for Ackbar's nostrils.

4 Cut out thin strips of beige felt and glue underneath the fold. These will be the fleshy bits that hang from Ackbar's mouth.

5 Cut a thick strip of black felt and glue inside the bag bottom's fold to make his mouth.

16

6 Trace the outline of the bag on the white felt. Cut out two pieces and glue them on the front and back of the bag as Ackbar's tunic. Cut and glue a thin strip of white felt to the top of the front and back of the tunic to make his collar. ◄

7 To make Ackbar's arms, roll a long tube of white felt and glue the edges together. Let dry. Then cut in half making two arms. Make hands from the beige felt and glue them inside the one end of each roll. Glue the arms to the side of Ackbar's body. ▼

ADMIRAL SACKBAR
PUPPET

8 Don't forget to cut out small squares of gray and black felt to make Ackbar's command insignia badges and glue them to his uniform.

BITH BAND SPOON PUPPETS

The Mos Eisley Cantina may not be the safest hangout, but Figrin D'an and his Bith band—the Modal Nodes—sure make it hoppin'!

WHAT YOU NEED

- Black beads
- Strong glue
- Wooden spoon
- Light beige, black, and gray pieces of felt
- Scissors
- Pipe cleaners
- Self-adhesive nylon fastening tape such as Velcro

How to Make Bith Band Spoon Puppets

1 Glue two black eye beads half-way between the tip of the spoon and where the handle meets the base.

2 Cut a tiny circle of black felt and glue it below the buttons for the mouth. Cut thin *C* shapes in the beige felt and glue on the face for the Bith's respiratory folds.

3 Wrap a pipe cleaner around the spoon handle so that your puppet looks like it has two arms.

4 Fold the black felt in half and cut out a long-sleeved shirt shape. Glue the front and back on the spoon handle with the pipe cleaner arms in between the shirt's sleeves. If you want to make the shirt extra-secure after you glue it in place, you can sew it as well.

5 Fold the beige felt in half and cut out two sets of hands with long fingers. Glue the fronts and backs of the hands to the ends of the pipe cleaners.

6 Using colored felt, make some instruments. They can be ones you recognize from this planet—or make up your own weird instruments! Stick nylon fastening tape such as Velcro on one side of the instrument and another piece on the hand of your puppet. Make four more puppets to complete the Modal Nodes band!

BITH
BAND
SPOON
PUPPETS

JAR JAR BINKS JEDI MIND TRICK DOLL

Whether you love or hate Jar Jar Binks, there's no denying that he's one klutzy Gungan. Here's a project that lets you make both good and embarrassing things happen to Jar Jar. Keep in mind that if you choose to make this Jar Jar Jedi Mind Trick Doll to be unkind to the Gungan, karma dictates that the same actions might happen to you! Poke at your own risk!

WHAT YOU NEED

- Jar Jar basic body, mouth, eyes, and ear patterns (see Appendix)
- Light beige, brown, and yellow felt
- Straight pins
- Scissor
- Pillow stuffing
- Needle and thread
- Fabric glue
- Orange pipe cleaner
- Small googly eyes
- Fabric pen
- White paper towel

How to Make a Jar Jar Binks Jedi Mind Trick Doll

1 Fold the light beige felt in half and pin the body pattern to it. Cut out the body pieces, hold them together with straight pins, and sew them together, leaving a space at the head. Fill the body with pillow stuffing. Sew shut.

2 Using the mouth pattern found in the Appendix, cut out two pieces to make the top and bottom of Jar Jar's mouth from light beige felt. Pinch the center of one of the pieces and whip stitch down the center to create a slight ridge. Repeat with the second piece. Cut out a long red tongue from red felt and attach to the inside of the bottom mouth with needle and thread or glue. Sew the bottom mouth to Jar Jar's head and then sew the top to his head, leaving a little bit of room between the two halves. Finish the mouth by gluing two brown felt circles for his nostrils to both sides of the top of his mouth.

3 Use the ear pattern to cut out four ears from light beige felt. Stuff and sew the set of ears (or—as the Gungans call them— haillu); then sew them to the back of the head.

4 Cut out a square of light beige felt, then wrap and glue it around a short piece of pipe cleaner. Make another one. These are Jar Jar's eyestalks. Glue the small googly eyes to the end or make your own eyes with yellow and black felt circles. Then sew the eyestalks to the top of the head.

JAR JAR BINKS JEDI MIND TRICK DOLL

5 Fold the brown felt and cut out a pants shape. Make this a bit bigger than Jar Jar's legs. Cut out the back and front of a tunic next. Sew to Jar Jar's body. ▶

6 In very small block lettering on the white paper towel, write single words or short phrases describing things that you would like to happen to Jar Jar. You can make the commands be good things, bad things, or a mix. I chose things that I wouldn't be too upset if they happened to me as well, such as "Hiccups" and "Chased by a Reek," as well as happy things: "Work Promotion" and "Make a Jedi Laugh."

7 Cut out the sayings and pin them onto Jar Jar's body. This way you can replace the sayings with new commands.

8 Use straight pins to poke the sayings on Jar Jar's body, or use him as a pincushion for your sewing needles!

Note: You can color the felt with an orange pastel to add color to Jar Jar.

CUDDLY BANTHA

Every Tusken Raider needs a trusty bantha to ride around the deserts of Tatooine. These elephant-sized creatures with long ram-like horns first showed up in *A New Hope.* It's easy to make your own cuddly bantha with some felt, stuffing, thread, and a lot of love.

WHAT YOU NEED

- Beige and light tan felt squares
- Sewing needle
- Tan thread
- Scissors
- Straight pins
- Pillow stuffing
- Chenille stems/pipe cleaners
- Chopsticks
- Buttons (for eyes)
- Beige fake fur
- Bantha action figure or images for reference

How to Make a Cuddly Bantha

1 Measure four beige felt squares into four rectangles. Sew the long edges together so you end up with one long piece of sewed felt. Then sew one end to the other so you make a rectangular cube.

2 Cut out a square of the beige felt and sew it carefully to the bottom of the cube. This will be one end of the bantha's body

3 Turn the fabric inside out and start stuffing.

4 Cut out another square piece of the beige felt and sew it carefully to the other end of the cube. Depending on which end you like best, this will be where the face will go, or the bantha's rear. The body should look like a cuddly loaf of bread.

5 Cut rectangle-shaped strips of the same beige felt and roll them into short tubes. Sew the edges together.

6 Stuff each tube and sew a circle onto each end. These four stuffed tubes will be the bantha's legs.

7 Cut diagonally on a piece of light tan felt to make two triangles. Roll and sew each one to look like an ice cream cone. Put a chenille stem in each one, then stuff. Use a chopstick to push the stuffing into the hard-to-reach parts of the cone. The wire in the stems will help you twist and position the bantha horns the way you want them to look.

8 Sew two black buttons on the face as eyes. Fold a long strip of felt back and forth and sew it to the head to make the bantha's mouth.

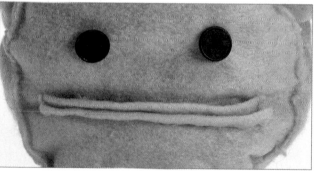

9 Before you sew the legs on the bantha, place the body on top of the legs to make sure they can hold its weight. If the legs are too tall, the bantha might topple over. Make the legs shorter by ripping the stitches out of the bottom of each leg, cutting it shorter, and re-sewing it shut.

23

craft continues on the next page

10 Sew the legs onto the bantha using a simple whip-stitch. It doesn't have to look pretty, but make sure the bantha can actually stand on the legs.

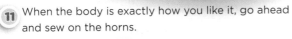

11 When the body is exactly how you like it, go ahead and sew on the horns.

12 Sew a rectangle of fake fur on top the body. Sew a wide strip of fake fur on his head between the horns to make his hipster bangs. Finally, sew on a triangle of fake fur under his mouth for his beard. Make a saddle if you want something for your Tusken Raider action figure to sit on—or let your bantha ride free! Now that you know how easy it is, make a whole herd of banthas!

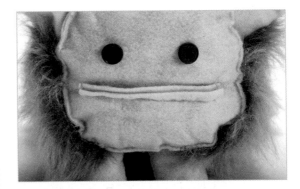

CUDDLY BANTHA

TOOKA DOLL

WHAT YOU NEED

- Tooka doll pattern (see Appendix)
- Light purple and beige felt squares
- Straight pins
- Scissors
- Sewing needle
- Tan, black, and purple thread
- Pillow stuffing
- Chopstick
- Buttons (for eyes)

How to Make a Tooka Doll

1 Make a copy of the Tooka doll pattern, or make your own by looking at a reference image of Numa's doll. Secure the pattern to two pieces of purple felt with straight pins. Then cut the felt.

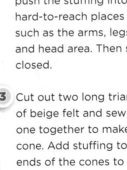

2 Sew the two pieces of purple felt together, but keep a hole open so you can turn the sewn piece inside out and then fill it with pillow stuffing. Use a chopstick to push the stuffing into hard-to-reach places such as the arms, legs, and head area. Then sew closed.

3 Cut out two long triangles of beige felt and sew each one together to make a cone. Add stuffing to the ends of the cones to fill them out. Then fit them over the headpiece and sew them down. Do the same to cover the hands and feet of the doll.

4 Cut out long strips of purple felt and sew them onto the head cones just like Numa's doll has in the episode.

5 Don't forget to sew on the button eyes so your doll can see you smile when you finish!

6 Now that you're done with the tooka doll, don't lose it . . . unless of course you need the help of a friendly clone trooper.

TOOKA DOLL

YODA FELT DOLL

Jedi Masters are fairly tricky to locate on this Earth, but with some craft supplies, a needle and thread—and a little patience—you can make your own cuddly Yoda felt doll. It's easy to make, plus it's fun!

WHAT YOU NEED

- Yoda doll patterns: body, Jedi robe front, Jedi robe back
- Green, brown, black, and gray felt squares
- Scissors
- Straight pins
- Sewing needle
- Green and brown thread
- Pillow stuffing or tissues
- Chopstick
- Glue
- Googly eyes
- Black embroidery thread or yarn

How to Make a Yoda Felt Doll

1 After cutting out the paper Yoda doll pattern pieces, place the body on top of the two green felt squares, and the Jedi robe pattern on the brown felt squares and cut each one out.

2 Secure the green felt body pieces together with straight pins. Then sew the felt together. Make sure to allow two spaces for stuffing the doll, one at the top and one at the bottom. ▶

3 Gently stuff Yoda's body using tissues or pillow stuffing. Use a chopstick to help move the stuffing into the harder-to-reach places of the doll. When the body is full, sew the openings shut. ▼

4 Glue two googly eyes on Yoda's face. Using black embroidery thread or yarn, sew on his nose and mouth. Or if you prefer, glue on a nose and mouth made from yarn or black felt.

5 Be sure the felt cutouts still fit the newly stuffed Yoda doll, and then sew the Jedi Master into his robe!

YODA FELT DOLL

Keep in mind that the back robe piece will be slightly bigger than the front piece to accommodate Yoda's stuffing. Add a piece of gray or tan fabric for his tunic to show underneath his robe. Cut any additional fabric around the sewing for a more tailored fit.

6 Have fun with your felt Jedi Master, and feel free to make Yoda his own set of accessories—a lightsaber, or a cane, or even a dwelling completely made from felt scraps!

HAMMERHEAD
SOCK DOLL

If you have a pair of old brown socks with holes in them, instead of sticking them back on your feet, make your own Hammerhead sock doll! Otherwise known to his Cantina pals as Momaw Nadon, this gentle Ithorian was sitting quietly in a darkened booth on the fateful day that Luke Skywalker wandered in.

WHAT YOU NEED

- Old brown or dark green sock
- Binder clips
- Scissors
- Pillow filler for stuffing
- Needle and thread
- Old T-shirt the same color as the sock
- Chenille stems/pipe cleaners
- Googly eyes
- Beige fabric (for his robe)
- Brown yarn (for his belt)

How to Make a Hammerhead Sock Doll

1. Luckily, socks already kind of have a built-in Ithorian hump. It's the heel! And because of their long necks, you can use almost the entire foot of the sock as the head. Use binder clips to estimate where you want to place your Hammerhead's eyes later.

2. Cut the ankle part of the sock into two parts for his legs. Start stuffing the sock with pillow filler. Fill it up

as if there's a fake foot in the sock. Then start sewing it up.

3. When you get to the bottom part of the sock that will be his feet, sew it closed—but fold the bottoms down like flaps. Then cut two slices in each flap for his toes and sew around them using a simple stitch, the way you did with the rest of the sock.

4. Now you need to make his arms and his long fingers. Cut two long rectangles from the T-shirt fabric about the length you want his arms from shoulder to fingertips. Then sew

the individual rectangles as though you're making two tubes. At the end of each tube, cut (as you did his feet) three slivers to make fingers, but make them wide enough so you can fill his fingers with pieces of chenille stems instead of stuffing. That way his fingers will bend and he can hold stuff like his staff.

5 Sew his arms to his body about where you think his shoulders will be. Also, scrunch up his neck a little so it bends like an S shape from the side. You can keep his neck in place by sewing the lower back of his lower head to his body.

6 For his eyes, cut out four ovals from the T-shirt fabric. Sew two of them together for each eye, leaving enough room to stuff them. Then fill them with pillow filler so they look like two lima beans and place a googly eye inside each one so it's barely visible. Sew around the fabric to make it more secure. That way he looks like he's squinting. Sew one on each side of his head.

7 Make some clothes for Momaw by draping beige fabric around him like a toga, or make a robe like Yoda wears from his felt doll craft. Use the brown yarn to make his belt! And make his staff by twisting two pieces of brown chenille stems together.

WASHCLOTH WAMPA

Wampa ice creatures may send shivers up your spine every time you think of one. After all, one wampa hung Luke Skywalker upside down in his cave on the snow planet of Hoth. But this craft project might show you the cuter and softer side of a wampa. Plus it's a great way to recycle white washcloths.

WHAT YOU NEED

- 3 white washcloths (or an old white towel)
- Scissors
- Needle
- White and brown thread
- Pillow stuffing
- White, red, and brown felt squares
- Paper and pencil for pattern making
- Straight pins
- Chopstick
- Glue
- Googly eyes or black buttons

How to Make a Washcloth Wampa

1. Place two washcloths on top of each other and cut off about three inches. Sew the sides of the washcloths together except for one side, so it looks like a small pillowcase.

2. Turn the sewn washcloths inside out and fill them with pillow stuffing. Sew shut. This will be the wampa's head and body all in one.

3 With the leftover washcloth material, roll two short cylinders for the legs.

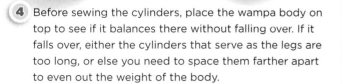

4 Before sewing the cylinders, place the wampa body on top to see if it balances there without falling over. If it falls over, either the cylinders that serve as the legs are too long, or else you need to space them farther apart to even out the weight of the body.

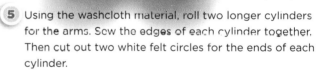

5 Using the washcloth material, roll two longer cylinders for the arms. Sew the edges of each cylinder together. Then cut out two white felt circles for the ends of each cylinder.

6 Fill the cylinders with pillow stuffing and leftover washcloth scraps. Sew a felt circle onto each end of the stuffed cylinders.

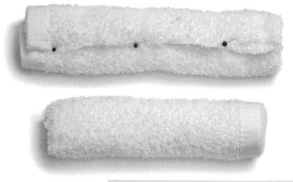

craft continues on the next page ➔

7 For the wampa's claws, cut out eight small triangles from the brown felt. Curl the two points of the triangle and sew or glue them together. Then sew four onto the bottom end of each arm.

8 Sew the stuffed arms (now with claws) to the body of the wampa.

9 For the wampa's horns, draw a moon crescent on a piece of paper and cut it out for your pattern. Put two pieces of brown felt together and pin the pattern on top. Cut two sets of crescents. Sew the sides of the crescents together except for one end on each. Using a chopstick, fill the crescents with pillow stuffing and sew shut.

10 Sew a stuffed crescent horn on each side of the wampa head.

11 For the wampa's mouth, cut out an oval of red felt. Next, cut out skinny triangles from the white piece of felt for the teeth. Glue the teeth to the red piece of felt, then glue the mouth to the wampa. Cut out thin white strips for the wampa's lips and glue them to the top and bottom of the mouth. Glue the mouth to the wampa's face and sew to make extra secure.

12 For the wampa's eyes, glue googly eyes or sew two black buttons to the face. Glue two thin strips of white felt above the eyes. You're finished!

WASHCLOTH WAMPA

DESIGN TIP

Attend Local Craft Fairs: Crafting has always been a major part of county fairs, and it seems more and more are popping up on a regular basis around the world. Look in your local paper or community online calendars to see when the next arts-and-crafts fair will be in your area. Take a friend and check out other artists' crafts for inspiration and ideas. Network with craftsters in your area to see if you can plan gatherings together when fairs aren't happening.

MOUSE DROID CAT TOY

Humans aren't the only ones who like to play with *Star Wars* toys. Treat your pet cat to a selection of homemade toys filled with catnip. By using fabric, felt, and a needle and thread, you can create a toy worthy of your favorite feline.

WHAT YOU NEED

- Scrap paper
- Scissors
- Felt squares
- Straight pins
- Needle and black thread
- Pillow stuffing
- Chopstick
- Dried organic catnip (available at pet stores)
- Black embroidery thread

How to Make a Mouse Droid Cat Toy

1 Look at pictures of a mouse droid from books and sketch the pattern freehand. Many droids are made of simple geometric shapes such as rectangles, squares, and hexagons. Cut out different shapes on the scrap paper to make patterns to cut from the felt squares.

2 Place the patterns you made on the colored felt squares and cut out. Most droids like this one are gray or black, but feel free to make your own from different colors if you want.

3 Be sure to secure the felt pieces with straight pins. Then sew the felt together by hand using a simple stitch. Allow a space for stuffing the droid.

4 Gently stuff the felt droid with tissues or pillow filler. Use a chopstick to help move the stuffing into the harder-to-reach places of the droid.

5 When the droid is almost full, make a cone funnel out of scrap paper and put one end in the opening of the droid. Carefully dump catnip into the funnel so it fills in the droid and mixes with the tissue or pillow filler.

6 Once you have the desired amount of catnip in the droid, sew the rest of it shut.

7 Add features to your droid using other bits of felt or by sewing on details with thicker embroidery thread. Make sure the pieces are sewn on well so your cat can't easily tear or chew them off.

8 To make wheels, roll two black pieces of felt, ½" wide, into two cylinder shapes and sew the edges. Cut four small circles from black felt and sew to each side of the two cylinders. Now sew the two cylinder wheels onto the bottom of the Mouse Droid body.

9 For the safety of your kitty, do not sew or glue on googly eyes, fake fur trim, or buttons. Experiment with other shapes to make more elaborate droids such as the gonk power droid, C-3PO, or R2-D2!

MOUSE
DROID
CAT
TOY

ROTTA THE HUTTLET SQUEAKY PET TOY

Jabba the Hutt's baby son Rotta is often called "Stinky" by Ahsoka Tano. But he might be called Squeaky once you've finished with this fun *Clone Wars* craft. Using sturdy fabric, old socks, embroidery thread, and a squeaker, you can make a fun toy for your dog or cat!

WHAT YOU NEED

- Paper
- Ballpoint pen
- Scissors
- Dark green denim or corduroy fabric
- Straight pins
- Sewing needle and dark-colored thread
- Old socks, fabric scraps, or pillow stuffing
- Dog toy replacement squeaker
- Thimble
- Catnip (if you want this to be a cat toy)
- Embroidery needle
- Embroidery thread—black, orange, and brown

How to Make a Rotta the Huttlet Squeaky Pet Toy

1. Draw a simple pear-shaped body and an arm on a piece of paper. Cut them out. These will be your sewing patterns.

2. For your fabric, you can use old green jeans or corduroy. Fold the fabric, or use a pant leg as it is and

secure the patterns using straight pins. You'll want two pieces of fabric for the front and back of Rotta's body and arms. You'll use the arm pattern twice. When you cut, leave some fabric around the pattern so you can sew it together with the pattern still pinned on.

3 Sew the pieces together using sturdy green thread, and be sure not to sew it entirely shut; you should be able to turn the fabric inside out.

4 Stuff Rotta's body and arms with pieces of scrap fabric, socks, or pillow stuffing. Be sure to place the squeaky toy inside Rotta's body. If you want this to be a cat toy instead of a doggy toy, add some catnip in with the stuffing. Then sew the pieces closed.

ANY SMALL SQUEAKER LIKE THIS WILL WORK WELL

5 Lightly draw on Rotta's eyes, nose, and long smile with a pen. This will be a guide for where you should sew using the embroidery thread.

6 Color in the eyes using the orange and yellow or brown embroidery thread, and use the black embroidery thread to sew an outline around the eyes, as well as for the nose and the mouth.

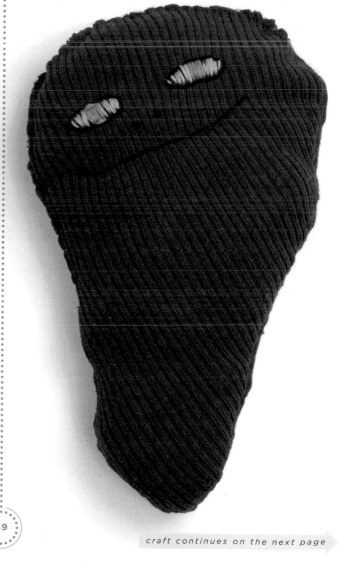

craft continues on the next page ➤

7 Now sew the arms to Rotta's body. Because the fabric is thicker than most, it might be hard to get the needle through, so use a thimble to help push the needle through the fabric. This is a pet toy, so you'll probably be sewing Rotta's arms back on quite a bit!

8 When you're done, you should have a smiling Huttlet looking back at you, waiting for you to hand him over to your dog or cat.

ROTTA THE
HUTTLET
SQUEAKY
PET TOY

USE
DIFFERENT
FABRICS FOR
A VARIETY
OF LOOKS

DESIGN TIP

Save That Sock! Holey socks shouldn't be exiled to the rag bin. Give that sock a better life as a doll or puppet! They also make ideal stuffing for toys and pillows.

STAR WARS AMIGURUMI
Sammi Resendes

Amigurumi is the Japanese art of crocheting to make cute stuffed dolls. Craftster Sammi Resendes created amigurumi dolls of Admiral Ackbar, Princess Leia, Yoda, Chewbacca, Han Solo, Boba Fett, Ahsoka Tano, and Darth Revan. There's even a Slave Leia! Resendes suggests to

fans who want to make their own dolls: "Amigurumi only requires you to know single crochet, and increasing and decreasing (which is just slightly modified single crochet)—so it's really easy to learn. Make sure you stuff the figures extra-tight, and weight them with something heavy (like beads or nuts from the hardware store) to make them stand up on their own."

HOME DÉCOR

2

Everyone's home should feel cozy, even if it's a humble hut on Dagobah or a minimalistic Star Destroyer. Show off your personality and your love for *Star Wars* with these easy-to-make crafts that are functional as well as fun! Stop pesky door drafts with a space slug, gaze at bounty hunters as you flick off the lights, and more!

SPACE SLUG DRAFT BLOCKER

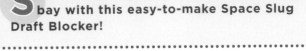

S ave on heating bills by keeping drafts at bay with this easy-to-make Space Slug Draft Blocker!

How to Make a Space Slug Draft Blocker

1 Fill the bottom of a large trash bag with sand. Roll the bag, fold over the opening, and tape it closed so it looks like a long space slug. ▼

2 Carefully stuff each end of the slug into a gray tube sock. Stretch out the sock so that there are no wrinkles.

3 Cut another sock lengthwise and use it to cover the middle of the slug, securing it shut with straight pins. Sew the middle together and then sew the piece to each end of the tube socks. Be careful not to pierce the bag inside with your needle.

WHAT YOU NEED

- Plastic garbage bag
- Sand
- Packing tape
- Gray tube socks
- Scissors
- Straight pins

- Sewing needle and gray thread
- Craft glue
- Googly eyes or black buttons
- White and red felt

4 Glue googly eyes or buttons onto one end of the sock. Make a mouth using a rect- angle of red felt—and don't forget to add multiple white triangles for its many teeth.

5 Place your slug on the floor by a drafty door—and don't let your *Millennium Falcon* near it!

SPACE SLUG DRAFT BLOCKER

DESIGN TIP

Thrift Store: You'll find products here similar to those at a dollar store, only older and in many cases funkier. This is where I go to buy clothes to refash- ion into something else. Many times you can get fleece fabric from an XXL fleece jacket that's much cheaper than buying the same material by the yard at a fabric store would be. Sweaters can be remade into leg warmers, coffee cup cozies, and hip wrist cuffs. Before you go to the craft store, come here first—you might find what you're looking for. You'll save money and make your crafts greener by up- cycling.

EWOK FLOWER VASE

Ewoks not only live in trees, but they use twigs for cooking, fighting, walking, and poking Han Solo in the ribs. Bring a little bit of Endor to your home with this super-easy-to-make flower vase.

WHAT YOU NEED

- Clean jar
- Scissors
- Tape
- Brown and beige felt
- Twigs
- Hemp twine
- Craft glue
- Googley eyes
- Beige pipe cleaner

How to Make an Ewok Flower Vase

1. Cover the outside of the jar with brown felt.

2. Gather twigs from outdoors. Brush off any dirt or bugs. Snap the ends of the twigs so they are all around the same height. The twigs should be slightly taller than your jar.

3. Interweave the twigs with the twine while gluing it to the brown felt covering the jar. Let dry.

4 Make an Ewok from felt and googley eyes. Give him a pipe cleaner spear and glue onto the vase.

5 Add water and pretty flowers.

DESIGN TIP

Raid the Recycling Bin: Clean glass jars, soda cans, plastic bottles, cereal boxes, and other food containers can come in handy for storage options, vases, and more. Start looking at your trash as possible treasure.

EWOK
FLOWER
VASE

CHEWBACCA TISSUE BOX COVER

Are cold and flu germs attacking your immune system like a pack of buzz droids? If so, you've probably been dragging along a tissue box wherever you go. Now you can have everyone's favorite Wookiee keep you company as you get better with this Chewie Tissue Box Cover!

WHAT YOU NEED

- Brown craft fake fur
- Tissue box
- Scissors
- Straight pins
- Needle and brown thread

- Large googly eyes (optional)
- Craft glue
- White, red, black, brown, and gray felt
- Black button or pom-pom

How to Make a Chewbacca Tissue Box Cover

1 First lay out your craft fur with the furry side down on a table, and place a tissue box at the end. You'll want to measure how much material you need by wrapping the box in the fake fur. Leave some room on top of the fabric so the fur can be folded down on the top of the tissue box.

2 Once you have an idea of how much fabric you need, cut off the extra material.

3 Attach the sides, as well as the folds on top of the box (leaving a slot for the tissues to get through), with straight pins. Sew the sides and top together. You can keep the fabric on the box for better control—just don't sew the cozy to the box!

4 For Chewie's face, make his eyes from white ovals and smaller black circles of felt, or glue on googly eyes. Cut an oval out of red or black felt for the mouth, then glue on white pointy triangles for teeth; glue this to his face. Lastly, glue on a black pom-pom or button for Chewie's nose.

5 Make Chewie's bandolier by cutting a long rectangle of

brown felt long enough to wrap around the body. Glue the ends together to make a sash. Cut small gray rectangles and glue to bandolier. Place around the body diagonally.

CHEWBACCA
TISSUE BOX
COVER

STAR WARS COLLAGE BOX

C an't find a paper clip when you need one? Need one place to put all your desk-supply odds and ends? Make your own handy *Star Wars* Collage Box, featuring images of your favorite characters, such as Yoda, C-3PO, R2-D2, Anakin Skywalker, Obi-Wan Kenobi, and Padme Amidala.

WHAT YOU NEED

- Images of *Star Wars* characters
- Scissors
- A recipe box or any small box with a lid
- Colored construction paper or felt
- Craft glue
- Glitter or glitter glue
- Glitter foam squares

How to Make a *Star Wars* Collage Box

1 The first thing you want to do is find *Star Wars* images that you'd like to print out, or cut out of a magazine to use to decorate your box. Better yet, draw your own *Star Wars* characters on paper to use for this project!

2 Next, trace around the lid and sides of your box onto the back of your images. Once you trace around the box sides and lids, cut out the images to paste on your box later. You can also trace the same measurements on colored paper or felt if you want this to be the box background instead. That way you can cut out your favorite characters and paste them on the construction paper or felt. It's up to you!

3 Glue the construction paper or felt to the box. Now glue your images to your box so they take up the whole box side, or overlap the images for a fun collage effect. If you want to make your box a little fancier, cut out and glue a felt lining to the inside and attach glitter foam to the inside bottom.

4 Don't forget the lid. Trace the lid on glitter foam board and cut it out and attach to the top of the lid. Wrap the sides of the lid in construction paper or felt. Now glue a fun *Star Wars* image on top of the lid.

5 Fill your box with smaller desk supplies, toys, collector cards, or whatever else you want to keep in one place.

STAR WARS
COLLAGE BOX

STAR WARS MARBLE MAGNETS

Want to make an Admiral Ackbar shrine on your fridge? Feel like turning your locker over to the dark side? Now you can make cool, one-of-a-kind *Star Wars* magnets by following the simple instructions below. Just gather up your favorite *Star Wars* images and get ready to have some crafty fun.

WHAT YOU NEED

- Small *Star Wars* images
- Craft glue that dries clear (silicone-based is best)
- White paper
- Scissors or ½" scrapbooking hole puncher
- Craft stick
- ½" round (strong) magnets
- Clear, flat marbles (usually found in the fake-flower area of the craft store)
- Clear nail polish

How to Make *Star Wars* Marble Magnets

1 Glue the images that you wish to use for your magnet to white paper. This will prevent the black magnet from being seen through your image. After it dries, cut your image out a second time now that it has a white paper backing. You will want it to be a circle about half an inch wide.

    Tip: If you don't want to use scissors, get a special craft hole puncher that punches half-inch holes (found in the scrapbook section of the craft store). Hole punchers make it easier for you to make a bunch of magnets at a time, but either method will work.

2 After you cut the image you want into a half-inch circle, set it aside. Next, put a small bead of glue on the craft stick. Then take one of the round magnets and carefully dab the glue onto one side with the craft stick, then place your cut-out image on top of the glue. You want your image to be facing up.

3 Now put a small amount of glue on the stick. This time, dab the glue in the middle of the flat side of a marble. Then place the glue-sided marble on top of your image on the magnet. Gently press down so that any air bubbles disappear.

Let dry. Paint the back of the magnet with clear fingernail polish so you won't leave any black marks from the magnets on the fridge or your locker.

STAR WARS
MARBLE
MAGNETS

DESIGN TIP

Cheap Art Makeovers: Look for cheap landscape paintings at local thrift stores, garage sales, and flea markets. Paintings of forests, rivers, and snowy scenes work best. Cut out images of AT-ATs, Ewoks, wampas, and other *Star Wars* characters you'd like to use. Or if you want, paint the characters and vehicles directly onto the painting. You'll want to match up the right characters and vehicles with their usual landscapes. Add a wampa or AT-AT to a winter painting, Ewoks or Wookiees to a forest scene, Yoda to a river painting. Or be wacky by adding characters to a painting for a more whimsical piece of art, such as Jabba in a picnic scene or R2-D2 in a meadow. Have fun making boring art into something uniquely yours.

HAN SOLO IN SOAPONITE

by Terri Hodges

Han Solo is a space pirate with some rather murky priorities. Help him clean up his act—and yours—with this easy soap craft.

WHAT YOU NEED

- Han Solo 3³⁄₄" action figure
- Rectangular soap mold large enough to accommodate 3³⁄₄" figure
- Melt-and-pour soap (white not clear)
- Large glass measuring cup with pour spout
- Soap fragrance and coloring (optional)
- Wooden stir sticks

How to Make Han in Soaponite

1 Place Han Solo in the mold lengthwise. Position him the way you want him to look and place the mold on a flat surface where it will not be moved after you pour. Soap solidifies fairly quickly, so you should set everything up before melting.

2 Melt the soap in the measuring cup according to the directions on the soap package, adding fragrance and coloring after the soap is melted if desired. Stir gently with stir sticks so bubbles do not form.

3 Pour the soap over Han, starting at his hands and working out so that everything has soap on it. Do not overfill. Han's hands should be sticking out of the mold slightly if you are emulating the movies.

4 Once the mold is filled, do not move for at least an hour, allowing the soap to set.

5 After twenty-four hours, you can pop the soap out of the mold, and clean up the galaxy.

HAN IN SOAPONITE

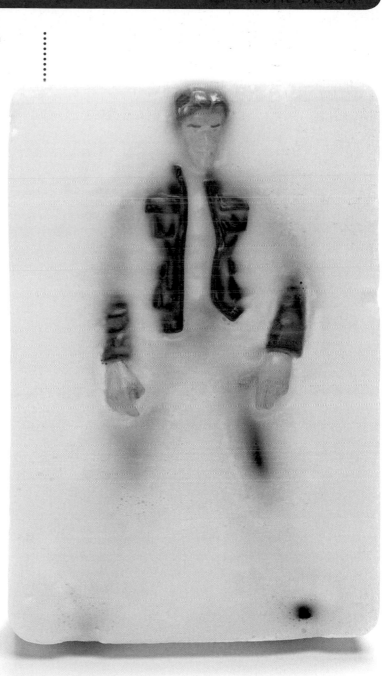

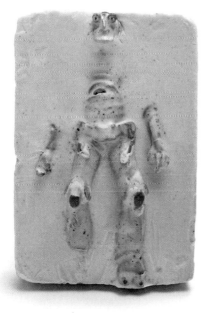

JAR JAR IN
SOAPONITE, TOO

JABBA THE HUTT
BODY PILLOW

Turn any room into Jabba the Hutt's palace with this cuddly body pillow craft. This is an ideal craft to use up old fleece blankets. When you're done, place Jabba on a bed or use him as an extra lounge pillow in your living room. Pretend you're Salacious Crumb and lean up against your new best friend while watching TV.

WHAT YOU NEED

- Pillows (three regular, two small, 1 large body pillow)
- String or white ribbon
- Sewing needle
- Thread (green, black, beige, orange colors)
- Large green fleece blanket
- Extra pillow stuffing
- Straight pins
- Scissors
- Beige fleece fabric or a beige sweatshirt
- Beige, black, and orange felt (or fleece)

How to Make a Jabba the Hutt Body Pillow

1 Stack up the pillows until they resemble the basic slug-body shape of Jabba the Hutt. Put the body pillow on the bottom, the regular-sized pillows in the middle, one of the small pillows on the top. Wrap the pillows together with string or white ribbon. Sew the pillow sides together so they stay in place. Sew the other small pillow to the end of the body pillow to elongate the tail.

2 Drape the green fleece blanket over the pillows until you're happy with how it looks. This is the part that you should take your time with. It doesn't have to be perfect. Folds in the fabric can look like Jabba's body wrinkles, so don't pull the fabric too taut. Tuck any extra fabric underneath. Add extra pillow stuffing inside the tail area to give it more shape and to fill in the gaps inside. Keep the fleece fabric in place with straight pins. Sew together.

3 Cut out a smaller slug-like shape from your beige fleece fabric, or you can use an old beige sweatshirt instead. This will be Jabba's face and inner body skin color. Keep fabric in place with straight pins then sew. Fleece is a great fabric to work with if you want to hide stitches. Your stitches will not stand out thanks to the fluffy texture of the fleece.

craft continues on the next page

Use felt for the facial features or fleece if you want it to be more durable. Cut two large ovals of beige felt, and then cut the ovals in half. These will be the top and bottom eyelids. Cut two smaller orange circles for the eyes. Cut two black almond shapes for the pupils. Cut two black comma shapes for the nose holes, and a large black strip for his mouth. Feel free to experiment with different

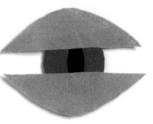

A FINISHED EYE

facial features if you want your Jabba pillow to look happy or more menacing. Keep facial features in place with straight pins then sew. Be sure to match the color thread with the color of your fabric.

5 You're finished! If you prefer to keep embellishing your Jabba the Hutt Body Pillow, make arms from the extra fleece material, or sew on an arm design using embroidery thread.

JABBA THE HUTT
BODY PILLOW

MOUNTED ACKLAY HEAD

If you want to give a room in your home that hunters'-lodge feel, but with a touch of *Star Wars,* make a Mounted Acklay Head for your mantel. In fact, you can use this project to make mounted trophies of all the creature heads from the Geonosian Arena scene in *Attack of the Clones.* This crumple-and-paste method of papier-mâché is from the genius monster maker Dan Reeder. He's very keen on using old bedsheets as well as the traditional newspaper method, which in fact makes a great skin-like texture.

WHAT YOU NEED

- **For the paste:**
- White flour
- Salt
- Large mixing bowl
- Water
- **For the taxidermy mount:**
- Plastic tablecloth
- Stack of old newspapers
- Masking tape
- Wire hangers
- Fimo or Super Sculpey (for the teeth)
- Cookie sheet
- Serrated knife

- Hot glue gun
- Old white bedsheet ripped into large and small strips
- White craft glue
- Dark green, light green, black, brown, white, and beige latex paints
- Paintbrushes
- Wire cutters
- Yellow marbles (or taxidermy animal eyes!)
- Acklay photos as reference

How to Make a Mounted Acklay Head

1 Before you do anything, put down a plastic tablecloth on your work surface. Now crumple up a sheet of newspaper into a ball. Keep adding crumpled newspaper sheets one over another until the ball is big enough to be the head of an acklay (about the size of a soccer ball); wrap this with tape. Make another ball just slightly smaller (this will later be used as a jaw).

2 Fold paper into two large triangles. Wrap paper around each triangle until each one is about ½" thick. These will be the ears.

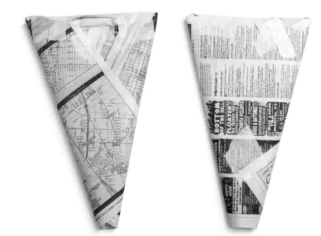

3 Bend a wire hanger so it's a long extended diamond. Twist pieces of newspaper into four long sections. Tape them side-by-side to the wire diamond, and add one long section in the middle to provide a "bump."

Wrap this structure in newspaper. This will be the crest of the acklay's head.

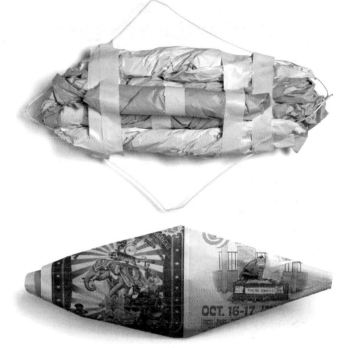

4 Make two wire loops and put them beside each other on an angle so that you form something of a 3-D diamond. Wrap newspaper around it and put aside. This will be your acklay neck.

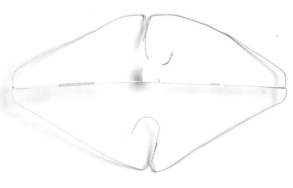

craft continues on the next page

5 Fold a sheet of newspaper several times over so it is about 2" wide and 6–7" long. This is the bit that hangs from his chin.

6 Now the messy fun part begins! Rip your newspaper at the folded end (it's easier to get a straight line that way) into wide strips. In fact, rip the newspaper into many sizes and widths to use for different parts of your acklay head. Set aside. Make the paste by pouring flour and a dash or two of salt into a bowl. Add water until the mixture reaches the consistency of a thick soup, like clam chowder. Mix with your hands. Now use your hands to put the paste onto the first big crumpled ball you made in Step 1.

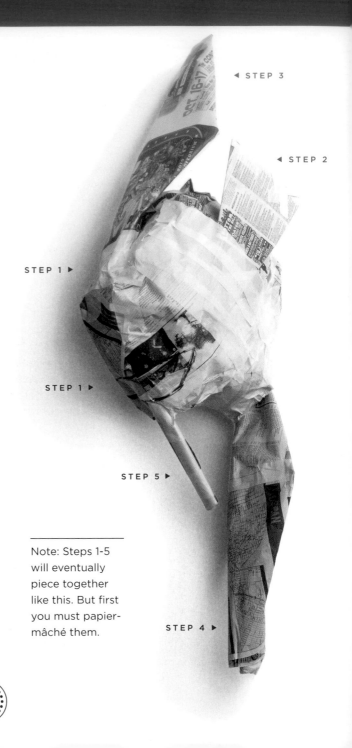

◄ STEP 3

◄ STEP 2

STEP 1 ►

STEP 1 ►

STEP 5 ►

STEP 4 ►

Note: Steps 1-5 will eventually piece together like this. But first you must papier-mâché them.

7 Add one piece of newspaper at a time, then add paste with your hands. Once that piece of newspaper is saturated with paste, add another piece. Continue until you have four or five layers. Do the same with the second smaller ball.

8 Using the same process, wrap strips of newspaper around the additional pieces you created in steps 2–5. Keeping your hands wet with the paste, squeeze out the bubbles trapped in the paper as you continue to add newspaper strips.

9 Place all the pieces in a warm place (near a heater) to dry. This may take a day or two. Be sure to turn the parts over after a day so they dry all over.

10 For the acklay's impressive set of chompers, roll a piece of Fimo or Super Sculpey between your fingers until it is an inch or two long and comes to a point. Make as many of these teeth as you need for the acklay. Make more than you think you'll need just in case. If you have too many teeth, you can always reuse them for another project. Bake the teeth on a cookie sheet according to the package's instructions.

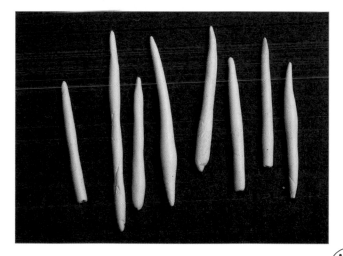

11 Once the head pieces are all dry use a serrated knife and cut the smaller ball in half. Stop before you go all the way through though, you want one side to hold the two halves together like a hinge. Using a hot glue gun, put a thin strip of glue on the outer edge of the ball where you cut into it. Add teeth to both halves, but alternate the gaps so the two halves of the mouth can close without bumping teeth. Don't worry about making the teeth look perfect. It's an acklay, not a beauty queen!

12 Dip two strips of bedsheet into white glue, fold them lengthwise, and place them above and below your acklay's teeth to look like gums. Once the teeth are done, attach the chin from Step 5 under the bottom set of teeth with tape and then strips of dipped bedsheet. Now cut a piece of cloth bigger than the jaw, soak it in glue, and place it inside the jaw. Do the same for the other jaw as well. Put these mouthparts somewhere warm to dry. This may take a couple of days, so be patient!

13 Once the jaws are dry, paint the inside dark green and light green going back and forth. Be careful to avoid the teeth so they stay white. Let dry.

14 Cut a hole in the large ball you made in Step 1 so that the back of the jaws can fit slightly inside. Use masking tape to secure them into the hole without falling in or out. Tape the ears to either side of the head, and the protrusions to the lower half. Next, place the large extended head plate onto the head and use masking tape to fix it into place. Do the same with the neck.

15 Dump your white craft glue into a large plastic bowl to soak strips of fabric, which you then place on your acklay so it looks like skin.

craft continues on the next page

16 Continue to cover the head of your acklay with strips of soaked bed-sheet. Remember to glue the yellow marbles onto the head right where you attached the extended head plate. Fold another piece of gluey bedsheet lengthwise and put it on top of and below the eye for lids. Add more gluey fabric strips to form a ridge above the eyes, as well as on top of the extended head plate.

17 Once you're happy with how your acklay head looks, put it somewhere warm to dry. This may take a few days considering how large it is.

18 Painting time! Use a light color of green all over the head except the underside of the jaw and the protrusions. Add dark green paint to the top of the head before the light green dries. Paint the underside beige and then add some light green. You want the colors to blend into one another so it looks more realistic. Be careful not to paint the teeth or eyes. Paint some black pupils onto the eyes. Let everything dry.

19 Glue the edge of the neck to a wooden mount or any piece of wood that's light enough to hang but strong enough to hold an acklay head. Let it dry, then hang it on the wall using a picture hook.

MOUNTED ACKLAY HEAD

HOLIDAY CRAFTS

3

Celebrate your favorite holidays like a Jedi Master with these easy and fun craft projects. Handmade gifts mean that you took the time to show someone how much you care for them. Creat one-of-a-kind decorations while having fun with family and friends.

WOOKIEE PUMPKIN

Inspired by Raphael Isaacs

Every Halloween fans carve and transform ordinary pumpkins into their favorite *Star Wars* characters. But instead of cutting a pumpkin, cover it with fake fur and make a Halloween tribute to Wookiees!

WHAT YOU NEED

- Magic marker
- Pumpkin
- Brown faux fur
- Glue gun
- Polymer clay like Sculpey
- Straight pins
- Aluminum foil
- Cardboard or empty raisin boxes
- Brown satin ribbon
- Large googly eyes
- Pink and black paint

How to Make a Wookiee Pumpkin

1 Using a black magic marker draw a line on your pumpkin from stem to the base. Draw a second line about one quarter of the width of the pumpkin away. If you're working with a very wide pumpkin you may want to make your sections smaller. Continue to do this until you've completely sectioned off the pumpkin.

2 Using sheets of aluminum foil, lay them on the pumpkin and fold or cut them to fit each section. These are now your fur templates or patterns.

3 Carefully lay the aluminum foil patterns on the fur and cut out the pieces of fur accordingly. Pay careful attention to match each pattern and piece of fur to correct panel on your pumpkin.

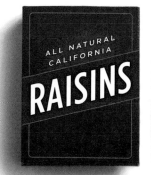

4 Using a hot glue gun, apply the fur sections to the pumpkin one at a time. Make sure there are no orange spots peeking out. Hold the fur in place while drying using straight pins.

5 Once the pumpkin is adequately furry-fied, move on to create Chewbacca's signature bandolier. Cut rectangles out of the cardboard or use empty small raisin boxes and wrap with aluminum foil.

ALL NATURAL
CALIFORNIA

RAISINS

craft continues on the next page

6 Glue the wrapped boxes onto the brown ribbon, then glue another piece of the ribbon on top of that. Glue ends together to create a sash for the bandolier. Glue the bandolier to the furry pumpkin.

7 Attach leftover pieces of the fake fur to the googly eyes and glue to pumpkin.

8 Shape a nose from the Sculpey and bake it according to the package's directions. Paint the nose, let it dry, then glue onto the pumpkin.

9 Finally, make the wookie's mouth out of red felt and glue teeth cut from white felt to it. Glue this to your pumpkin and you are done.

DESIGN TIP

Real or Fake: Use a fake pumpkin instead of a real one. You won't need to worry about your craft rotting and you can use it for years to come.

LET THE WOOKIEE PUMPKIN WIN

Raphael Isaacs

Using various types of faux fur, glue gun, Sculpey, aluminum foil, cardboard, satin ribbon, and googly eyes, fan Raphael Isaacs transformed a boring pumpkin into a Wookiee warrior. "We were determined to make the pumpkin look as Chewbacca-like as possible, which as everyone knows requires copious amounts of fur," Isaacs says. "Also, with the right tools, covering a pumpkin in fur is a lot easier than carving it."

HANUKKAH DROIDEL

Celebrating Hanukkah often includes playing the traditional game of dreidel. A dreidel is a four-sided top with a symbol on each side that represents a word. Put together, these words are the Hebrew phrase *Nes Gadol Hayah Sham*—which translates as "A Great Miracle Happened There."

In this *Star Wars* variation, the dreidel and the droid R2-D2 combine to make a Droidel! Make a copy of this paper craft pattern and create your own for the holidays.

WHAT YOU NEED

- Droidel pattern (see Appendix)
- Glue or tape
- Card stock, manila folder, or cardboard
- Scissors
- Small pencil or straw

How to Make a Hanukkah Droidel

1 Copy the droidel pattern found in the Appendix and glue it to a thin piece of card stock, manila folder, or cardboard, like the kind from a cereal box.

2 Once the glue is dry, carefully cut it out along the edges (including the flaps). Also cut out R2-D2's circle dome.

3 Cut out the circle in the body top. This is where the small pencil or a straw will go—so you can spin the droidel like a top.

4 Fold along the lines on the inside, then glue or tape where the flaps tell you. Do the top part last.

5 Fold the extra R2-D2 circle top into a wide cone and place it on top of the droidel with glue or tape. Make sure the holes line up.

6 Now stick a small pencil or a straw through the holes you cut at the top and push down until it rests on the bottom of the droidel.

7 Now you're ready to play!

HANUKKAH DROIDEL

How to Play the Dreidel Game

To begin the game, each player should have fifteen objects to use as prize tokens. You might choose chocolate coins in gold wrappers (gelt) as tokens, or another candy that's handy. Each person puts one object in the middle. Then everyone takes turns spinning the dreidel. Whichever symbol is faceup after spinning determines what each person should do.

 Nun means "*nicht*" or "nothing." If the dreidel lands on nun, you do nothing. The next person spins the dreidel.

 Gimel means "*gantz*" or "all." If the dreidel lands on gimel, you take the goodies everyone put in the middle. Everyone then adds another coin in the middle to continue the game, and the next person spins the dreidel.

 Hei means "*halb*" or "half." If the dreidel lands on hei, you take half of what's in the middle, and the next person spins the dreidel.

 Shin means "*shtel*" or "put in." If the dreidel lands on shin, put two goodies in the middle. The next person spins the dreidel.

The game ends when one player has all the goodies!

STAR WARS ACTION FIGURE WREATH

Deck the halls with your broken and extra action figures by using them in this festive wreath for the holiday season. It's a great way to get your toys in the Yuletide spirit!

WHAT YOU NEED

- Foil Christmas garland wreath or fake evergreen wreath
- Broken or extra action figures
- Green acrylic paint
- Paintbrushes
- Green glitter paint
- Green twine
- Green ornament hooks
- Red ribbon

How to Make an Action Figure Wreath

1 Unwind the foil garland wreath to the size you prefer. You can also substitute a larger fake evergreen wreath, available at most craft stores. Gather the action figures and pieces you want to use.

2 Paint all the action figures you plan to use with green acrylic paint. Let them dry and then add a coat of green glitter paint to give them extra sparkle. Let your figures dry again.

3 Place the painted action figures where you want them on the wreath. Experiment with different placement for the best look.

4 Tie the action figures to the wreath either by using green twine or by twisting green ornament tree hooks around your figures.

5 Use a piece of red ribbon to tie a bow for the base of your wreath.

6 Feel free to use bigger action figures and vehicles as a topping for extra fun!

7 This wreath is a traditional green, but you can have fun making different themed wreaths featuring your figures, such as all-white for Hoth or red for Mustafar!

STAR WARS
ACTION
FIGURE
WREATH

MISTLE-TIE FIGHTER

Decking the halls with boughs of holly isn't the only way to have fun celebrating the Christmas holiday. Hang traditional mistletoe with this easy-to-make felt TIE fighter.

WHAT YOU NEED

- Pencil
- Manila folder
- Scissors
- Black, gray, and white felt
- Thin cardboard
- Quick-drying fabric glue
- Chenille stems/pipe cleaners
- Table tennis or small styrofoam ball
- Wooden drink stir stick or thin dowel
- Fresh or plastic mistletoe
- Red ribbon
- White thread or clear fishing wire

How to Make a Mistle-TIE Fighter

1 First draw a hexagon (a six-sided figure) on a manila folder and cut it out to use as your TIE fighter solar panel pattern.

2 Cut four hexagons out of black felt, and two from the thin cardboard.

3 Glue the black felt hexagons to both sides of your cardboard hexagons.

4 Cut the pipe cleaners and glue them onto the hexagons in a crisscross and straight-across pattern, just as it appears on a TIE fighter solar panel. Use an image of a TIE fighter solar panel from books as a reference.

Be sure to glue pipe cleaners around the edges of the solar panels, too. Cut out a smaller hexagon from white felt to glue in the middle of each side of the solar panels.

6 Wrap and glue a piece of white felt around the ball and wooden stick and glue at the end. Allow the glue to dry.

7 Use quick-drying fabric glue to glue each end to the middle of a solar panel. This is where you must practice Yoda-like patience by allowing the glue to dry on one solar panel before you attach the other. Let the glue dry completely.

8 Next, cut out a circle of gray felt and a smaller circle of black felt to glue on top to make the cockpit window. Cut out thin slivers of gray and an even smaller gray circle to go in the middle of the window. After it dries, glue the finished window to the middle of the cockpit area of the TIE fighter.

5 Begin the cockpit assembly by creating a hole in each side of the table tennis or styrofoam ball. Push the wooden stir stick or dowel through the ball and trim it so it is even on both sides. Secure it with a bit of glue on each side.

9 Wrap a pipe cleaner stem around the arms of the TIE fighter and below it to attach your mistletoe bundle underneath.

craft continues on the next page

10 Tie a pretty red ribbon around the pipe cleaner and stems of your mistletoe as an added festive touch. Tie a piece of white thread or clear fishing line to each arm of the TIE fighter and make two loops. Then tie the loops together at the top with another loop of thread to serve as the main hanging loop, which will properly support your TIE fighter.

11 Hang in a doorway, but remember that Christmas tradition states you have to kiss anyone standing underneath the mistletoe! So look out for lurking Wookiees!

MISTLE-TIE
FIGHTER

MILLENNIUM FALCON BED

Kayla Kromer

Crafty fan Kayla Kromer just found another reason to hit the snooze button thanks to her comfy *Millennium Falcon* bed! Working without a pattern, and through trial and error, she made this one-of-a-kind light-up bed. "The bed is a 1970s round mattress," Kromer ex-plains. "The sides, cockpit, and triangular pieces are foam. The down comforter my mom donated. The duvet and everything is covered in gray flannel. The sheets are just white sheets modified for a circular mattress. I used a variety of fabric paints for the detail work. My favorite bed details are the smuggling areas (for my keyboard, mouse, and glasses), the detachable (for Jedi) plushy radar, [the fact that] the cockpit can hold figures and the fitted sheet is an interior map, and the lights in the front and back."

STAR WARS SNOW GLOBE

Snow globes are fun to play with, but even more of a blast to make. It's a great way to recycle small glass jars and display extra *Star Wars* miniatures you might have handy.

Instead of fake snow, use white glitter to make a globe, such as the one which re-creates the snowy tundra-like planet where the Talz species lives (in the "Trespass" episode of *The Clone Wars*). But you can also use an AT-AT or wampa ice creature figure to make a Hoth scene, or switch to green glitter and make a Dagobah scene, or use your imagination to make your own scene.

WHAT YOU NEED

- Small glass jar with lid (baby food jars work great)
- Acrylic or spray paint
- Strong glue (not water-soluble)
- Plastic bottle cap

- *Star Wars* toy miniature—such as a Talz figure
- Distilled water
- Glycerin or clear dish soap (optional)
- Chunky silver or white glitter

How to Make a Snow Globe

1 Clean out a small glass jar. Paint the jar lid using acrylic or spray paint ▶

2 Using strong craft glue (that's not water-soluble), secure your *Star Wars* miniature to the bottle cap to serve as a stand. That way you'll be able to see your miniature better in the globe. Then glue the bottle cap to the inside center of the jar lid. Let this dry.

3 Fill your jar almost to the top with distilled water. Add a few drops of glycerin or clear dish soap to keep the glitter from falling too fast. Screw the lid on to make sure you have enough water to fill the jar, but not so much that it spills. Then add silver or white glitter—or both—to the water. Place glue along the rim of the jar opening and inside the lid, then screw tightly shut. Let it dry overnight.

4 Turn the glitter globe right-side up and shake, shake, shake!

USE OTHER
CHARACTERS
TO BUILD
YOUR OWN
SNOW GLOBE
COLLECTION

STAR WARS
SNOW GLOBE

NATURE & SCIENCE CRAFTS

4

All Jedi understand the importance of planets and their environments. Learn about Earth by making crafts utilizing supplies you find in your own backyard.

DAGOBAH CARNIVOROUS PLANT HABITAT

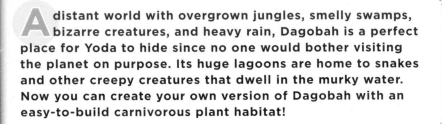

A distant world with overgrown jungles, smelly swamps, bizarre creatures, and heavy rain, Dagobah is a perfect place for Yoda to hide since no one would bother visiting the planet on purpose. Its huge lagoons are home to snakes and other creepy creatures that dwell in the murky water. Now you can create your own version of Dagobah with an easy-to-build carnivorous plant habitat!

WHAT YOU NEED

- Large plastic bottle or glass vase
- Polished pebbles
- Garden charcoal (optional)
- Sphagnum moss
- Carnivorous plants such as Venus flytraps or a non-carnivorous plant such as an air plant (see Plant Tips on page 90)
- Extra pebbles
- Small *Star Wars* toys (optional)

How to Make a Dagobah Carnivorous Plant Habitat

1. Use a glass vase or cut off the top of a large plastic bottle so you can use the bottom for the habitat. Start with a one-and-a-half-inch layer of small pebbles on the bottom of the container.

2 Cover the pebbles with a thin layer of loose charcoal, which will help keep the water in your garden from smelling stale.

3 Now top this with multiple layers of sphagnum moss.

5 Decorate it by adding extra rocks, pebbles, and moss if you want. Give it some *Star Wars* flair by adding a small Yoda or Luke Skywalker figure.

4 Next, carefully add the Venus flytraps and other plants to the moss.

craft continues on the next page

6 Once everything is in place, keep the habitat in a well-lit area near a big window—but don't put it directly in the sun, or you'll fry all your live plants and moss!

Plant Tips

- Use only distilled water—carnivorous plants hate tap water because of the minerals and added elements.

- Do not overwater your terrarium! Since there's no drainage hole for the water to get out, you'll want to add only enough water that the soil is barely moist. Never have a pool of water in the bottom pebble layer.

- Carnivorous plants don't need to be fed. As much as you wish you could feed them your leftovers, these plants do fine catching small bugs on their own.

- Venus flytraps often die back in winter and come back thriving in spring. So don't be too quick to throw out the plant if you see some brown leaves.

- Don't play with your plant too much. Even though it's fun to have the flytrap close on your finger, it will do so only a few times before it cannot close again and falls off the plant.

Read more about carnivorous plants online or find a book in your local library.

Alternative Habitat: If carnivorous plants aren't your thing, you can do this exact same project using air plants, which are very low-maintenance. Mist the plants with distilled water once a week to keep them happy and thriving.

STAR WARS ROCK BUDDIES

Collect smooth stones whenever you go for a walk. Think of which characters or creatures the stones remind you of as you pick them up. Put the stones in a basket until you're ready to paint.

WHAT YOU NEED

- Smooth stones
- Plastic tablecloth or newspaper
- Pencil
- Acrylic paints
- Paintbrushes
- Clear nail polish

How to Make *Star Wars* Painted Rock Buddies

1. Pick out and clean the stone you'd like to paint. Use elongated stones for the heads of battle droids, heart-shaped stones for Yoda, and wide ovals for astromechs.

2. Place newspaper or a plastic tablecloth down on your work surface before you start painting.

3. Paint your rock the color of your character of choice—yellow for C-3PO, white for R2-D2, green for Yoda, and so on.

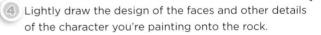

4. Lightly draw the design of the faces and other details of the character you're painting onto the rock.

⑤ Paint in the details with the acrylics. Let dry.

⑥ Coat the painted rock with clear nail polish on one side. Allow it to dry, then coat the other side.

⑦ The painted rock buddies make excellent planter decorations or even paperweights for your desk.

DESIGN TIP

You're a Crafting Star! Instead of just making a craft for your own amusement, teach others how you made your project with a crafting tutorial. Write out your steps and take photos to show the process. Or better yet, shoot a video tutorial and post it online for others to enjoy. Pretend you have your own DIY network where you're the star!

WOOKIEE BIRD HOUSE

Wookiees live in beautiful houses in the trees on Kashyyyk. Take some inspiration from Chewbacca's home and make a delightful dwelling for the birds in your own backyard.

WHAT YOU NEED

- ½-gallon milk or juice carton (cleaned)
- Acrylic paints
- Paintbrush
- Scissors
- Craft sticks or twigs
- Spray on sealant

- Strong crafting glue
- Googly eyes
- Unsalted sunflower seeds, various birdseed

How to Make a Wookiee Bird House

1. Cut a hole midway in the carton for birds to go in and out. Paint the inside black if you want.

2. Paint the milk carton brown and paint the cap black (this will be Chewbacca's nose). Let it dry.

3. Glue twigs or craft sticks side by side to the outside walls of the carton. Snap sticks to fit smaller spaces. Let dry.

4. Paint it brown like Chewbacca's fur. Let dry.

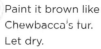

5. Now you need to give Chewie a face. Make the opening for his mouth by first painting a black outline around it. Then once it's dry paint teeth on the top and bottom. Paint Chewbacca's bandolier on the bottom.

6. Spray the painted carton with sealant. Let dry.

7. Glue on googly eyes or paint eyes on the top on each side above his nose.

8. Put birdseed into your bird house and place outside so your feathered friends can find their new deluxe Wookiee home.

DESIGN TIP

Go Online: Thanks to the Internet, crafty folks have been sharing ideas and encouraging one another to find their artistic side online. Visit sites like Craftzine.com and Craftster.org to meet other craftsters who are always more than happy to give tips, teach basic sewing skills, and more. It's fun to see what others are doing with the same kinds of materials you have around the house. Start your own crafting blog to show off your current projects and get feedback from others.

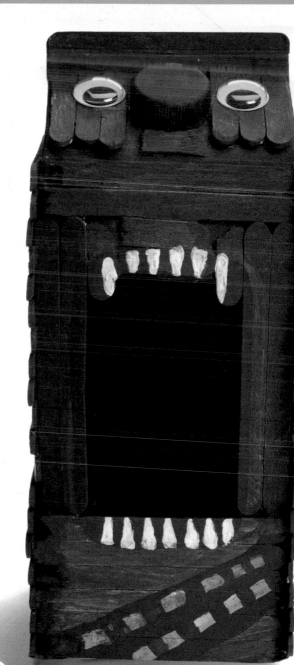

WOOKIEE BIRD HOUSE

EMPEROR APPLETINE DOLL

If an apple a day keeps the doctor away, an Emperor apple doll might do the opposite—at least in Anakin's case.

WHAT YOU NEED

- A green apple
- Paring knife
- Bowl
- Water
- Lemon juice
- Salt
- Black beads
- Pipe cleaners
- White cotton balls
- Light beige and black felt
- Glue
- Black fabric
- Polyester fiberfill

How to Make an Emperor Appletine Doll

1. Peel and core the apple. With a paring knife, make a U shape in the middle side of the apple; this will eventually be the nose.

2. Carve away the edges of the apple by cutting toward the lines of the nose, making the nose profile more profound.

3 Continue to carve away apple from under the nose, under the cheeks, and where you want the eyes.

4 Cut a large slit for the mouth. Also cut less deep lines on the forehead and around the eyes. You should be able to see more of the face taking shape on the apple.

5 Fill a bowl with water, a bit of lemon, and a couple of tablespoons of salt. Soak your apple for a couple of minutes, then put it on a rack to dry.

6 Depending on the humidity in a room, the apple head could take longer to dry. Try putting it near a heater, or in an area that gets consistent dry heat. You'll know the apple head is ready when it feels spongy yet dry. Feel free to reshape parts of the face at this stage.

craft continues on the next page

7. Stretch out a cotton ball so it resembles white hair. Fold a pipe cleaner over the cotton ball and twist the pipe cleaner at the ends. Pull through the middle of the apple so the cotton ball is on the top of the head.

8. Bend the pipe cleaners into loops for arms and legs, making a crude body shape. Twist onto the pipe cleaner already in the apple doll head.

9. Cut out a basic body shape from the black felt. Place on top the pipe cleaners with polyfill and glue shut. Cut out hand shapes from beige felt and glue to the ends of the pipe cleaner arms.

10. Stick beads sideways for eyes into the head.

11. Wrap black fabric around the body and glue (or sew) it into place. Wrap another piece of black fabric around the head and glue into place.

12. Make a cane out of black pipe cleaner or give him a red light-saber (see instructions on page 8). Emperor Appletine is now ready to make some trouble.

EMPEROR APPLETINE DOLL

EMPEROR APPLETINE DOLL
WITH LIGHTSABER

AT-AT HERB GARDEN

Transform plastic containers sitting in your recycling bin and a simple planter into an AT-AT indoor garden that grows herbs and flowers instead of squashing Rebel scum.

WHAT YOU NEED

- Rectangular plastic planter
- Roll of duct tape
- Hammer and nail
- Strong epoxy glue
- Wooden dowel, about 5" long
- 4 small plastic soup bowls
- 4 cylindrical chip containers (empty and clean) with lids
- Self-adhesive nylon fastening tape such as Velcro dots
- 2 square mini baskets
- Plastic pudding container (empty and clean)
- 2 straws
- Perlite
- Organic potting soil
- Fresh herbs like thyme, rosemary, chives, lavender (optional indoor low-light plant substitutes: flowers and ferns)

How to Make an AT-AT Herb Garden

1. To make the main body of the AT-AT, cover your rectangular plastic planter with duct tape. Puncture a few holes with a nail on the bottom of the planter for drainage. Puncture another hole in the middle of one end of your planter and glue one end of the wooden dowel so it's sticking outside of the container.

② Glue a plastic soup bowl to the open end of the cylindrical chip container. Repeat this step for the other three chip containers. Let dry. Then cover each in duct tape. These will be the legs of your AT-AT. Cover the plastic chip container lids with duct tape and, using the Velcro dots, stick each lid midway up one "leg" to serve as the "knee-caps" of the AT-AT.

③ Glue the two baskets together to make the head of your AT-AT. Cover in duct tape. Poke a hole in one end (to attach the other end of the wooden dowel when you put the AT-AT body parts together).

④ Cover the pudding container with duct tape. This is the neck of your AT-AT. Poke a hole through the bottom (for the wooden dowel to go through when you assemble the AT-AT). Duct-tape the neck to the head. Make sure the hole in the head and the neck line up.

⑤ Time to assemble the AT-AT! Stand up your AT-AT legs and position them under the body of the planter to see where the ideal placement will be to allow the planter to remain upright. Experiment with different leg placements, then glue the tops of the legs to the bottom of the planter. Let dry. Secure further with duct tape.

craft continues on the next page

6. Put glue on the wooden dowel that's sticking out of the planter body. Place the neck and head on the dowel so that the dowel is also inside the head. This will support the head of your AT-AT so it doesn't droop. Cover with duct tape.

7. Cover the two straws with duct tape, then tape them to either side of the head of your AT-AT to represent the guns.

8. Add perlite (for soil drainage) to the bottom of the planter, then potting soil. Add some herbs and flowers.

9. Position the planter indoors by a sunny window. Alternatively, you can skip step 8 and keep potted houseplants in the planter instead.

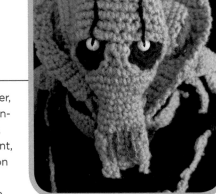

CROCHETED GENERAL GRIEVOUS

Amber Mendenhall

After learning how to crochet, crafty fan Amber Mendenhall made *Star Wars* scarves and dolls—but it's her General Grievous craft that's truly impressive. His body is completely crocheted, with a sewn cape. He is very large at about three feet tall. "General Grievous is really darn complicated," Mendenhall says. "There are lots of pieces and a complete structure inside of him. He took quite a lot of time—altogether probably about six full days. I worked on him for three months on and off. I have made Imperial and Rebel symbol scarves, an Admiral Ackbar, a stormtrooper, Yoda, and General Grievous. At the moment, I'm working on a Boba Fett. After that, I'm going to make a Chewbacca. I love being creative. It's really cool to be able to use some yarn and stuffing and make a really incredible piece of art. The cool thing about *Star Wars* characters is that there are so many one can re-create. Eventually, I want to make most of the alien races and major characters. Crafting is a great way to use your creative juices, and it's super-easy to pick up."

AT-AT HERB
GARDEN

BOSSK BEAN PORTRAIT

All bounty hunters deserve a portrait created with dried beans and glitter, and Bossk is no exception. Pay special tribute to everyone's favorite Trandoshan with this fun craft project. Feel free to experiment with different beans and materials to make a one-of-a-kind work of art.

WHAT YOU NEED

- Printout image of Bossk (see Appendix)
- Scissors
- Mod Podge glue
- Toothpicks
- Paintbrush
- Light cardboard or thin wood
- Dried beans (kidney, split pea, black, pinto, lentil)
- Almond slivers (for his teeth)
- Colored sand (optional)
- Glitter glue and paint
- Beads (optional)
- Magnets (optional)
- Medium wooden box for frame (optional)
- Black felt (optional)

How to Make a Bossk Bean Portrait

1. Before you get started, glue your Bossk printout to a thin piece of cardboard or wood canvas. This is so your art won't warp as you glue beans to it.

2. Use the art as a guide for where to glue your beans. For Bossk, use split peas for his green, lizard-like skin; black beans for his eyes and mouth; and slivered almonds for his teeth!

3. Experiment with different kinds of beans for the look you want. Orange lentils, green lentils, and red kidney beans work best for Bossk's stylish outfit.

(4) Once you're done gluing all the beans, glue on colored sand for the background. Or use glitter for extra sparkle. Also feel free to adorn the art with beads and other trinkets. Let everything dry overnight.

(5) Attach picture hanging hardware to the back of the portrait so you can hang it. To make your art extra-special, glue magnets to the back four corners of your portrait and then four corresponding magnets to the inside of a long wooden box or shadow frame. Then glue a large piece of black felt to the box over the magnets. Once this dries, you can place your portrait on the magnets in the box—it will look like it's floating in the frame!

BOSSK BEAN PORTRAIT

STAR WARS STYLE

5

Be a Force-sensitive fashionista with these
stylish crafts. Make your own jewelry,
add embellishments to your wardrobe,
and reconstruct T-shirts into something
cooler then they were before. The
galaxy is your own fashion runway!

STAR WARS CHARACTER RINGS

Show off your *Star Wars* style by making these fashionable rings featuring your favorite characters from *Star Wars.*

WHAT YOU NEED

- Small *Star Wars* images
- Clear, flat domes (usually found in the fake-flower area of the craft store)
- Glue that dries clear
- Scissors
- Metal ring backings (available at craft stores)
- Glitter glue (optional)

How to Make *Star Wars* Character Rings

1 Set a glass dome over your image to see where you want it placed. Keep in mind the dome will slightly enlarge your image because of its shape. Then place a tiny bit of glue on the flat side of the dome and press it on top of your image. Don't worry about the glue making your image cloudy. The glue will dry clear. Let this dry.

Note: Another way to do this is to cut out the image first, then glue it the same way to the flat side of the dome. Either way is fine.

2 Once the glue is dry, cut around the image to get rid of the extra paper around your dome.

3 Put a small amount of glue on the ring backing and press the flat side of the dome to the glue. Hold it for a few seconds until it's secure, then let it dry completely.

4 Experiment with making different kinds of rings. Add glitter glue to your glass glue for an extra sparkle. Paint on top of the glued image before you glue it to the backing. Draw your own images and give your friends and family custom-designed jewelry made by you!

DESIGN TIP

The Dollar Store Is Your Friend: This is the place to visit for cheap houseware items, electronics, candles, clothes, party supplies, figurines, kitchenware, washcloths, towels, ice cube trays, toys, stationary, bandannas, fake flowers, marbles, and more.

STAR WARS
CHARACTER
RINGS

STAR WARS T-SHIRT BLANKET

by Amanda Jean Camarillo

If you have a collection of *Star Wars* T-shirts that don't fit, consider cutting them up to make this comfy blanket.

WHAT YOU NEED

- *Star Wars* T-shirts
- Cardboard cutout of blanket square size (6x6")
- Sharpie pen
- Fabric scissors
- Straight pins
- Sewing machine (or you can hand-sew)

How to Make a *Star Wars* T-Shirt Blanket

1 Gather together your *Star Wars* shirts. The best shirts to use have good designs all over, so you can get more squares out of each one.

2 Use your square cardboard piece and use your Sharpie pen to mark the places you want to cut out for your blanket squares. Try to fit as much detail as you can into each square, and try to get as many squares from one shirt as possible.

3 Once you have some squares marked, go back with your fabric scissors and cut out all your squares.

4 Count how many squares you have cut out and cut out the same number of squares from the backs of the shirts (with no design) for the back of your blanket—you can either use all one color or make a checkered back.

5 Next, lay out your squares to the shape you want your blanket, with the non-design squares under the design squares.

6 Pin the design squares to the non-design squares that are under them.

7 Now it's time to sew! Take your pinned squares and sew them from corner to corner. Then lay them out again in blanket form.

8 Take your first horizontal row and sew the squares edge-to-edge together, leaving ¼" from the edge—for the frilly part.

9 Once all your horizontal lines are sewn, sew the rows together, leaving ¼" from the edge again—more frillies.

craft continues on the next page

10 When you have sewn all your rows together and you have one blanket, sew once around the whole thing.

11 Take your fabric scissors and make little cuts in the fabric you left on the edges to create the frillies.

12 Now curl up under your blanket and watch your favorite *Star Wars* movie.

STAR WARS
T-SHIRT
BLANKET

STAR WARS T-SHIRT CRAFTS

Amanda Jean Camarillo _____

What do you do with piles of *Star Wars* T-shirts that don't fit anymore? Crafty fan Amanda Jean Camarillo discovered that old T-shirts make the perfect material to turn into one-of-a-kind blankets, T-shirt dresses, and even lamp shades. "My favorite *Star Wars* crafts to make are when I'm able to take old T-shirts and make them into dresses or other clothing," Camarillo says. "They always turn out so cute and unique. But the most meaningful craft that I've made was the blanket that I made for my boyfriend out of almost 100 of his old *Star Wars* shirts. The amount of time that went into it and the meaning and history behind each shirt made it extra special for us both. When you're crafty with *Star Wars* and the Force on your side it makes it even better. Plus with all the other cute crafty fans out there we can inspire each other and make the *Star Wars* world very cute and unique."

R2-D2 CROCHETED BEANIE

by Reynalyn Camoras

Now you can show your astromech pride while keeping your noggin warm with this cute R2-D2 crocheted beanie. This is a loose-fitting beanie designed to fit most adults. It measures approximately 22 to 24 inches around the bottom edge or head circumference. If you want a smaller, tighter hat, try a smaller hook and/or lighter yarn such as DK or sport-weight.

YARN

- 3.5 ounces (100g) silver-gray worsted-weight yarn
- 2 ounces (57g) royal blue worsted-weight yarn
- Small amounts of black, red, and off-white worsted-weight yarn

GAUGE

- Gauge = 12 stitches and 6 rows dc = 4"

ADDITIONAL ITEMS

- G-hook
- F-hook
- Yarn needle
- Stitch markers
- Black, red, and off-white buttons (optional)

Notes

- The beanie is formed by alternating gray and blue stitches to form the design on R2's dome. Change colors by pulling new color through the last two loops of the current-color stitch. Read ahead before finishing stitches so you will know when to change colors.

- Carry unused colors under stitches of current color. Do not finish off unless otherwise indicated.

- The large central square featuring R2-D2's main "eye" will be used as a reference point and abbreviated as "LCS."

- The hat is worked from the crown down to the open edge. Directions such as "right" and "left" refer to your point of view as you work each round.

- Be patient. Don't be afraid to pull out stitches. Use an R2-D2 action figure, a paper model, or movie photo stills as reference so you will understand how the pattern is forming. (Keep in mind that design variations occur on R2 products.)

Pattern Abbreviations

- st(s) = Stitch(es)
- ch = Chain Stitch
- dc = Double Crochet
- dec = Decrease
- incs = Increase
- sc = Single Crochet
- sl st = Slip Stitch
- yo = Yarn Over
- dc2tog = YO, insert hook in st indicated, pull up a loop, YO, pull through 2 loops, YO, insert hook in st indicated, pull up a loop, YO, pull through 2 loops, YO, pull through 3 loops (counts as 1 stitch)

How to Make an R2-D2 Crocheted Beanie

W/G-hook and blue yarn, ch 4, join with sl st in first ch to form ring.

Round 1: Ch 1, work 9 sc in ring. Join w/sl st to first st. 9 sc.

Round 2: Ch 1, 2 sc in each st, switching to gray to finish last st. Join w/sl st to first st. 18 sc.

Round 3: W/gray ch 1, sc in same st, ch 1, *sc in next st, ch 1*, repeat from * to * around, switching to blue on last sc. Join w/sl st to first st. 18 sc and 18 ch-1 spaces.

Note: Ch-1 spaces count as stitches. You may work into them or under them on this round.

Round 4: W/blue ch 3 (counts as dc), dc in next 2 sts, *w/gray dc in next st, w/blue dc in each of next 5 sts*, repeat from * to * 4 times, w/gray dc in next st, w/blue dc in last 2 sts. Join w/sl st to first st. 36 dc.

Round 5: W/blue ch 3, dc in same st, dc in next 2 sts, *w/gray dc in next st, w/blue dc in next 2 sts, 2 dc in next st, dc in next 2 sts*, repeat from * to * 4 times, w/gray dc in next st, w/blue dc in last 2 sts. Join w/sl st to first st. 42 dc.

Round 6: W/blue ch 3, dc in same st, dc in next 3 sts, *w/gray dc in next st, w/blue dc in next 3 sts, 2 dc in next st, dc in next 2 sts*, repeat from * to * 4 times, w/gray dc in next st, w/blue dc in last 2 sts, switching to gray to finish last st. Join w/sl st to first st. Finish off blue. 48 dc.

Round 7: W/gray ch 1, sc in same st, sc in next st, 2 sc in next st, *sc in next 2 sts, 2 sc in next st*, repeat from * to * around. Join w/sl st to first st. 64 sc.

Round 8: W/gray ch 3, dc2tog beginning in same st and finishing in next st, dc in remaining sts. Join w/sl st to first st. 64 dc.

Note: On round 9, you will begin the LCS, the big blue square in the middle of R2's dome.

Round 9: W/gray ch 1, sc in same st and next 24 sts, w/blue sc in next 8 sts, drop blue to side. (You will carry it across to right edge of LCS on subsequent rounds.) W/gray sc in remaining sts. Join w/sl st to first st. 64 sc.

Note: When you reach the LCS, carry the blue yarn across to the right edge of the LCS and finish the last gray sc, drop the gray yarn, st over both the carried blue and dropped gray yarn. After the last blue st, switch back to gray and drop blue. Use this technique for each round of the LCS.

Round 10: W/gray ch 3, dc2tog beginning in same st and finishing in next st, dc in next 23 sts, carry blue from previous round to right edge of LCS and use it to finish last gray dc, 2 dc in next st, dc in next 6 sts, 2 dc in next st, finish with gray, drop blue yarn, dc in remaining sts. Join w/sl st to first st. 66 dc.

Note: Read entire paragraph before crocheting round 11.

Round 11: This round is all sc, following the colors of the previous rounds, gray in gray, blue in blue. You will also

craft continues on the next page

work 9 evenly spaced incs—4 before the LCS, 5 after. If you find it difficult to evenly space the incs as you crochet, then visually divide the section into fourths or fifths and place st markers where you want to add the incs.

W/gray ch 1, sc w/4 evenly spaced incs before LCS. Carry over and drop yarn as in previous rounds. W/blue sc in each blue st. W/gray sc w/5 evenly spaced incs in remaining sts. Join w/sl st to first st. 75 sts.

Round 12: W/gray ch 3, dc2tog beginning in same st and finishing in next st, dc in next 27 sts, carry and drop yarn as in previous rounds, w/blue dc in next 9 sts, 2 dc in next st, w/gray dc in remaining sts. Join w/sl st to first st. 76 sts.

Note: In round 13, you will work 8 incs, 4 before the LCS, then 2+2 after.

Round 13: Place a marker in the 19th gray dc to the left of the LCS. W/gray ch 1, sc w/4 evenly spaced incs to the LCS, carry and drop yarn as in previous rounds, w/blue sc in next 11 sts. Drop blue yarn but carry it under sts. W/gray sc w/2 evenly spaced incs until you reach the marker. W/blue sc in next 2 sts, drop and carry blue yarn, w/gray 11 sc in next 10 sts, w/blue sc, w/gray sc, w/blue sc, w/gray 4 sc in last 3 sts. Join w/sl st to first st. Finish off blue. 84 sts.

Round 14: Place a marker 5 sc to the right of the right edge of the LCS. This is where you will begin the divided rectangle. W/gray ch 1, sc w/3 evenly spaced incs until you reach the marker; w/blue sc in next 4 sts, w/gray sc in next st, w/blue sc in next 11 sts, finish off blue. W/gray sc w/2 evenly spaced incs before the blue bar (the 2 consecutive blue sc), and sc w/1 evenly spaced inc after the blue bar. Join w/sl st to first st. 90 sts.

Note: Here's where the fun begins. On round 15, you will focus on all the lovely vertical and horizontal rectangles on R2's dome. There will be much switching of color, but no more increases. Unless noted, you will crochet 1 stitch in each stitch. To speed things up, directions will be given by number, color, and type.

Round 15: W/gray ch 3, dc2tog beginning in same st and finishing in next st, 3 gray dc, 10 blue sc, 3 gray dc, 8 blue dc, 2 gray dc, 2 blue dc, 1 gray dc, 1 blue dc, 2 gray dc, 1 blue dc, 1 gray dc. You should have reached the LCS. W/blue 11 blue dc. Continue with 6 gray dc, *2 blue dc, 1 gray dc*, repeat from * to * twice, 6 blue dc, 1 gray dc, 3 blue sc, 1 gray dc, 6 blue dc, 1 gray dc, 8 blue dc, 2 gray dc. Join w/sl st to first st.

Round 16: W/gray ch 1, 5 gray sc, 1 blue sc, 5 gray sc, 4 blue sc, 3 gray sc, 8 blue sc, 2 gray sc, 2 blue sc, 1 gray sc, 4 blue sc, 1 gray sc. You should have reached the LCS. Working in the back loop only, 11 gray sc. Working in both loops, 6 gray sc, *2 blue sc, 1 gray sc*, repeat from * to * twice, 6 blue sc, 1 gray sc, 1 blue dc, w/gray dc2tog in same st, 1 blue dc, 1 gray sc, 6 blue sc, 1 gray sc, 8 blue sc, 2 gray sc. Join w/sl st to first st.

Round 17: W/gray ch 3, dc2tog beginning in same st and finishing in next st, 3 gray dc, 10 blue dc, 3 gray dc, 8 blue dc, 2 gray dc, 2 blue dc, 1 gray dc, 1 blue dc, 2 gray dc, 1 blue dc, 2 gray dc, 2 blue dc, 1 gray dc, 6 blue dc, 7 gray dc, *2 blue dc, 1 gray dc*, repeat from * to * twice, 6 blue dc, 1 gray dc, 1 blue dc, gray dc2tog in same st, 1 blue dc, 1 gray dc, 6 blue dc, 1 gray dc, 8 blue dc, 2 gray dc. Join w/sl st to first st.

Round 18: W/gray ch 1, 18 gray sc, 8 blue sc, 2 gray sc, 2 blue sc, 1 gray sc, 4 blue sc, 2 gray sc, 2 blue sc, 1 gray sc, 6 blue sc, 7 gray sc, *2 blue sc, 1 gray sc*, repeat from * to * twice, 6 blue sc, 1 gray sc, 3 blue sc, 1 gray sc, 6 blue sc, 1 gray sc, 8 blue sc, 2 gray sc. Join w/sl st to first st.

Round 19: Do not carry blue on this round. Drop it to the side, but do not finish off. W/gray ch 1, sc in each st. Switch to blue to finish last gray sc. Join w/sl st to first st.

Round 20: W/blue, ch 1, hdc in first and remaining sts. Switch to gray to finish last st. Join w/sl st to first st. Finish off blue.

Round 21: W/gray ch 1, sc in each st. Join w/sl st to first st.

Round 22 is optional: Repeat round 21 for a deeper hat.

Note: Round 23 tightens the hat. You may continue with the G-hook, but if your hat is very loose, you may switch to an F-hook or omit the ch-1 spaces on alternate repeats. Experiment with the final round until the fit is to your liking.

Round 23: W/gray ch 1, turn hat so wrong side is facing, *sc in next st, ch 1, skip next st*, repeat from * to * around. Join w/sl st to first st. Finish off.

Embellishments—those three little gray tubes and the three circles: R2-D2 has three main circles or "eyes" on his dome—the large black one, the small red one below it, and the off-white one on the back. Instructions for eye making are below, but if you are tired of all this, sew on buttons in the size and color of your choice and skip this step entirely!

craft continues on the next page

Large Black Eye

- G-hook

Round 1: W/black ch 2. Work 6 sc in second chain from hook. Join w/sl st to first sc. 6 sc.

Round 2: Ch 1, 2 sc in each st. Join w/sl st to first sc. 12 sc.

Round 3: Ch 1, 2 sc in first st, 1 sc in next st, *2 sc in next st, 1 sc in next st*, repeat from * to * around. Join w/sl st to first st. Leave a long end for sewing. Finish off. 18 sc.

W/wrong side of eye facing up, sew eye to center of LCS.

Small Eye

- F-hook

Note: Make two: one red and one off-white.

Round 1: Ch 2. Work 6 sc in second ch from hook. Join w/sl st to first sc. Leave a long end for sewing. Finish off. 6 sc.

W/wrong side of eye facing up and using photos as a guide for placement, sew eye to hat.

Those Three Little Gray Tubes

The front tube, from which Princess Leia's message sprang, is called a holoprojector. For simplicity's sake, I will refer to all of them as holoprojectors. This step is also optional. No one's going to notice if you omit the holoprojectors except maybe other R2 beanie makers.

- F-hook (to make a holoprojector that will remain upright, crochet tightly with the smallest hook size you can stand; an F-hook is used here)

Note: Make three.

Round 1: W/gray ch 2. Work 6 sc in second ch from hook. Join w/sl st to first sc. 6 sc.

Round 2: Ch 1, 2 sc in each st. Join w/sl st to first sc. 12 sc.

Round 3: Ch 1. Turn circle over. Working in back loop only, sc in each sc. Join w/sl st to first sc. 12 sc.

Round 4: Ch 1, sc w/3 evenly spaced decs. Join w/sl st to first sc. 9 sc.

Round 5: Ch 1, sc w/1 dec. Join w/sl st to first sc. Finish off and leave a long end for sewing. 8 sc.

Weave yarn end through st to outside edge of bottom circle of tube. Using photos as a guide for placement, sew holoprojectors to hat.

You're done! Now put on your beanie and go forth to astound the world with your geeky, droidy, astromechy crocheted goodness!

R2-D2 CROCHETED BEANIE

Reynalyn Camoras

One of the most famous fan-made crafts has to be the R2-D2 crocheted beanie by Reynalyn Camoras. "I placed a crocheted beanie for an interactive R2-D2," Camoras explains. "It fit so well that I realized I could follow the design and proportions and crochet an R2-D2 beanie. Also, this was the only affordable and non-life-threatening way I could achieve my dream of becoming part droid. There are many ways to enjoy *Star Wars:* collecting, costuming, gaming, et cetera. Crafting is another way fans can play in the *Star Wars* galaxy. You can create items based on well-known characters or objects while adding your own tweak or twist to make them unique."

R2-D2
CROCHETED
BEANIE

EWOK FLEECE HAT

Make this adorkable and warm Ewok hat using fleece and fake fur!

WHAT YOU NEED

- Dark brown fleece
- Scissors
- Needle and thread
- Light brown yarn
- Black fake fur
- Pillow stuffing

How to Make an Ewok Fleece Hat

1 Cut enough fleece material to make a hoodie that drapes down off your shoulders. Think of it as a poncho for your head.

2 Cut out a hole for your face to peek though. You want it to be a bit big so your chin isn't resting on the bottom of the face hole.

3 Sew hat pieces together on top and sides. Sew X marks with the yarn above the face hole, just like Wicket the Ewok's hat.

4 Cut out two large heart shapes from the piece of fake fur and cut down the middle to make two sets of heart halves.

5 Sew the edges of each half together and fill with pillow stuffing; then sew shut. These are your Ewok ears. Sew them to either side of the top of the hat.

6 Put on the hat and go stalk Han Solo.

EWOK
FLEECE
HAT

FIVE THINGS TO DO WITH A *STAR WARS* T-SHIRT

L et's face it: We all have at least one *Star Wars* T-shirt that doesn't fit quite right. It's either too small to wear without ripping further, or so big it might as well be an extra tent. Here are five super-easy projects you can do to make something even cooler from a shirt that's at the bottom of your closet right now.

T-SHIRT NAPKINS

WHAT YOU NEED

- colorful cotton napkins
- Pencil
- Thin cardboard (such as that from a cereal box)
- Scissors
- *Star Wars* T-shirt
- Needle and thread

How to Make T-Shirt Napkins

1 Trace the cotton napkin on the thin cardboard and use this as your template.

2 Using the cardboard template, cut squares from your T-shirt. Make sure you get in the design or cut around the image on your T-shirt to sew onto the napkin.

3 Sew the T-shirt square to the napkin. By doing this, you're making an extra-strong yet absorbent reusable napkin that will look fab at your next dinner party.

T-SHIRT
NAPKINS

T-SHIRT THROW PILLOW

WHAT YOU NEED

- *Star Wars* T-shirt
- Scissors
- Straight pins
- Needle and thread

- Pillow stuffing or pillow form
- Decorative ribbon, rickrack, or pom-poms

How to Make a T-Shirt Throw Pillow

1 Cut out a large square from the front and back of your T-shirt.

2 Flip the squares so the T-shirt design is facing in. Pin together. Sew all the edges closed except one.

3 Turn right-side out and fill with pillow stuffing or a pillow form (to save time).

4 Sew the last edge closed.

5 Sew decorative ribbon, rickrack, or pom-poms alongside the edges of the pillow.

T-SHIRT THROW
PILLOW

T-SHIRT EYE SOOTHER

WHAT YOU NEED

- *Star Wars* T-shirt
- Scissors
- Straight pins
- Needle and thread
- Dry rice
- Lavender

How to Make a T-Shirt Eye Soother

1 Cut six-by-eleven-inch rectangles from the front (with the design) and back of the shirt.

2 Flip the rectangles so the T-shirt design is facing in. Pin together and sew all the sides except one.

3 Turn right-side out and fill with dry rice and lavender. Sew shut.

4 Rest on your eyelids and relax!

T-SHIRT EYE SOOTHER

T-SHIRT TOTE

WHAT YOU NEED

- *Star Wars* T-shirt
- Scissors
- Fabric to line the bag (*Star Wars* fabric is ideal)
- Straight pins
- Needle and thread
- Material for the straps (such as fleece)

How to Make a T-Shirt Tote

1 Cut out two large rectangles from the front and back of the shirt. Cut rectangles of the same size from the fabric to line the bag.

2 Pin the fabric to the back of both T-shirt squares and sew the edges together.

3 Flip the rectangles so the T-shirt design is facing in. Pin together. Sew together all sides except one.

4 Turn right-side out. Fold the inside edge and hem.

5 Cut two wide strips from the extra liner material or fleece. Fold over and sew the edges on both pieces. Sew both strips into the opening of the bag to serve as handles.

DESIGN TIP

Crafts and Arts Supply Store: Your local craft store not only has everything you could possibly need for crafting under one roof, but many of them offer classes on how to do everything from knit to reupholster old chairs. Sign up for your store's mailing list to see what events and sales are on the horizon.

T-SHIRT
TOTE

T-SHIRT PUNK FIX
AND T-SHIRT TOTE

T-SHIRT PUNK FIX

WHAT YOU NEED

- *Star Wars* T-shirt
- Scissors
- Iron
- Fusible interfacing
- Straight pins
- T-shirt that fits well
- Needle and thread
- Colored safety pins

How to Make a T-Shirt Punk Fix

1 Cut out the design from your *Star Wars* T-shirt.

2 Iron the fusible interfacing onto the back of the design.

3 Pin the design to the new shirt and sew it on using different-colored thread for effect.

4 Add safety pins to the shirt to give it a punk-rock fashion sense.

DESIGN TIP

Fuzzy Wuzzy Crafts: Fake crafting fur comes in all shades and styles. It's an ideal material for making Wookiee, Wampa, and Ewok crafts, but it also hides sewing mistakes rather well. Many craft stores sell remnants of fake fur in their clearance sections, so look for a sale before you buy. If you can't find fake fur, materials like shag carpet, old mohair sweaters, and even extra-fuzzy towels will work in a pinch.

APPENDIX

Here you will find the patterns you need to make the various puppets and dolls in this book along with images you can use to make marble magnets and rings. The droidel image and a painting of Bossk are both here as well, and Bossk is just waiting to have beans glued to him. Don't want to cut the pages from your book? Make a color photocopy of the Appendix pages you need or you can visit www.star-wars.suvudu.com and download a PDF of this section that you can print out.

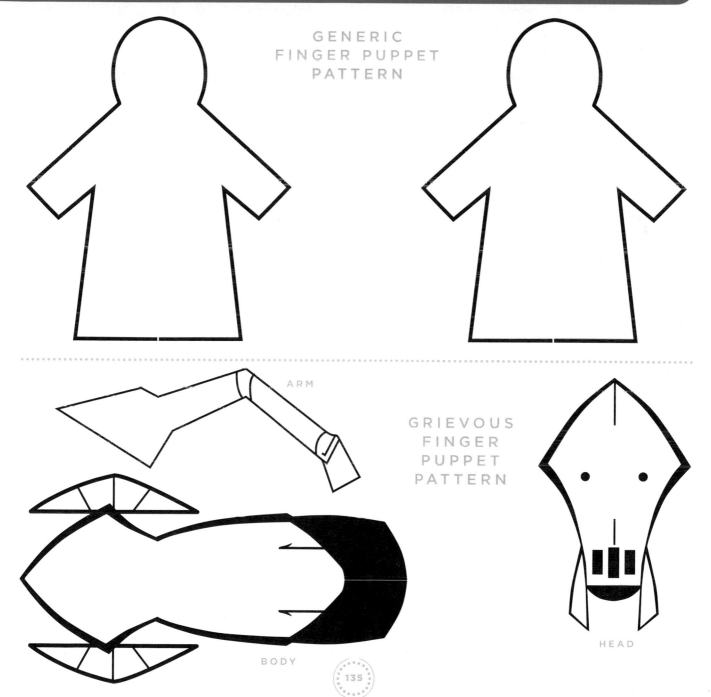

GENERIC
FINGER PUPPET
PATTERN

GRIEVOUS
FINGER
PUPPET
PATTERN

ARM

BODY

HEAD

135

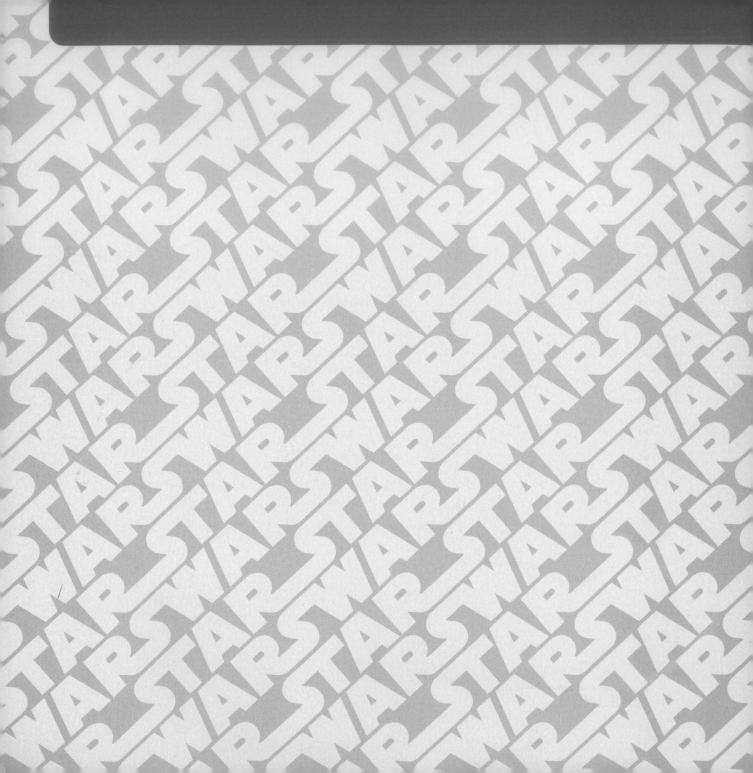

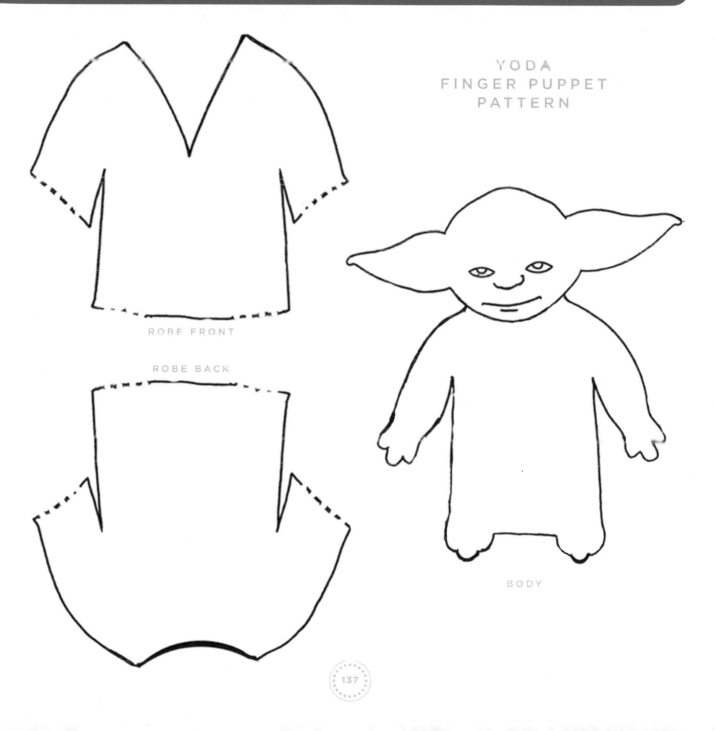

ROBE FRONT

ROBE BACK

BODY

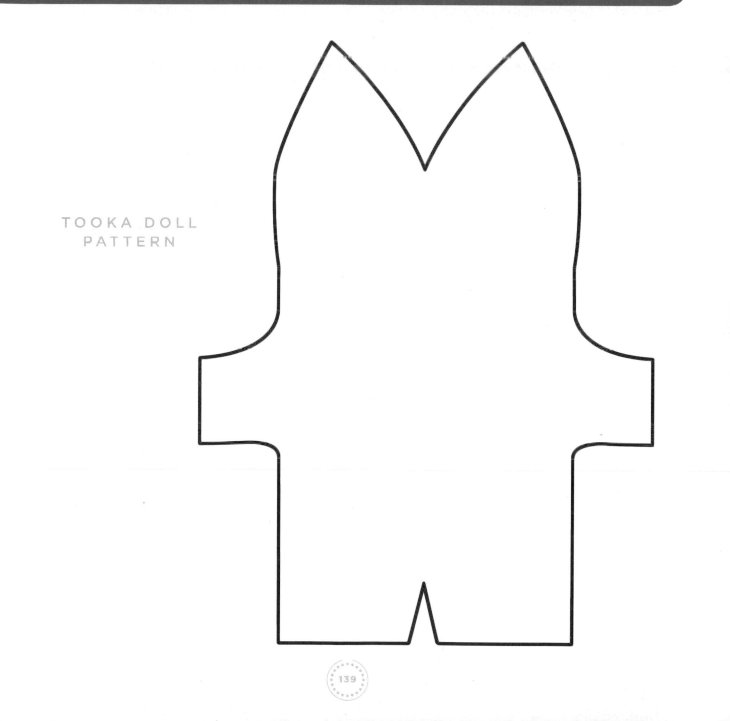

TOOKA DOLL
PATTERN

YODA DOLL
PATTERN

BODY

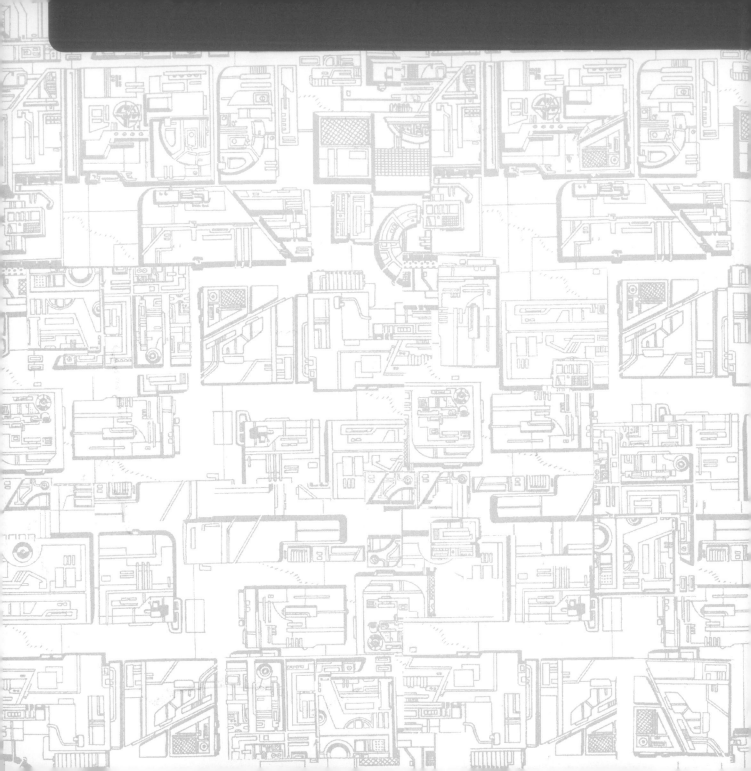

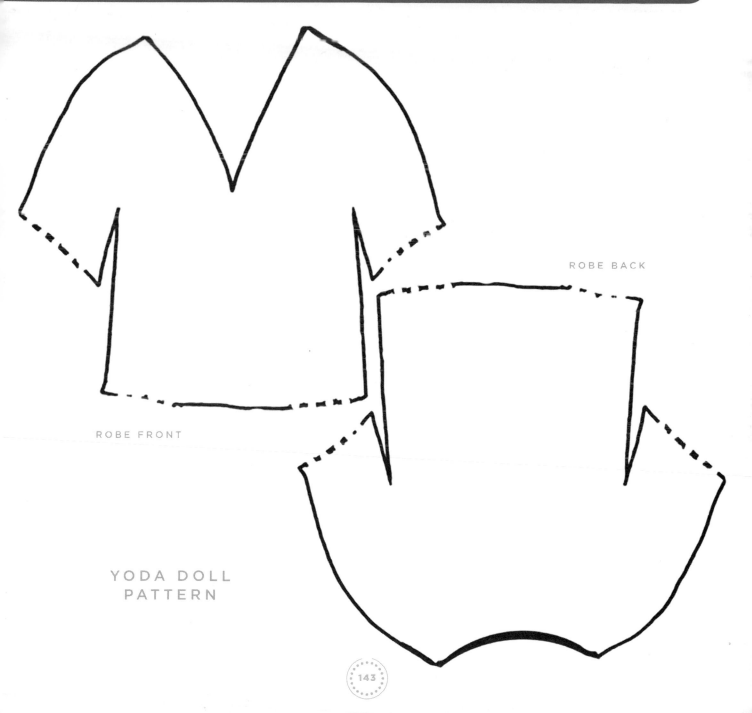

ROBE BACK

ROBE FRONT

YODA DOLL
PATTERN

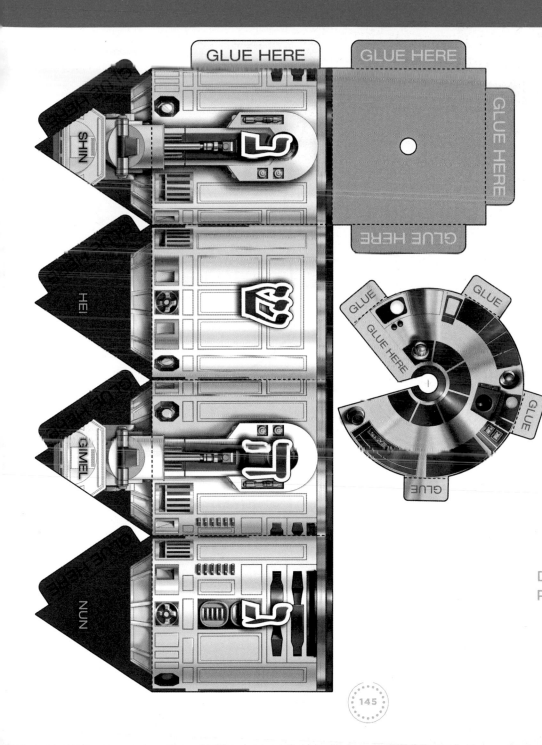

GLUE HERE

GLUE HERE

GLUE HERE

GLUE HERE

SHIN

HEI

GIMEL

NUN

GLUE

GLUE

GLUE HERE

GLUE

GLUE

DROIDEL
PATTERN

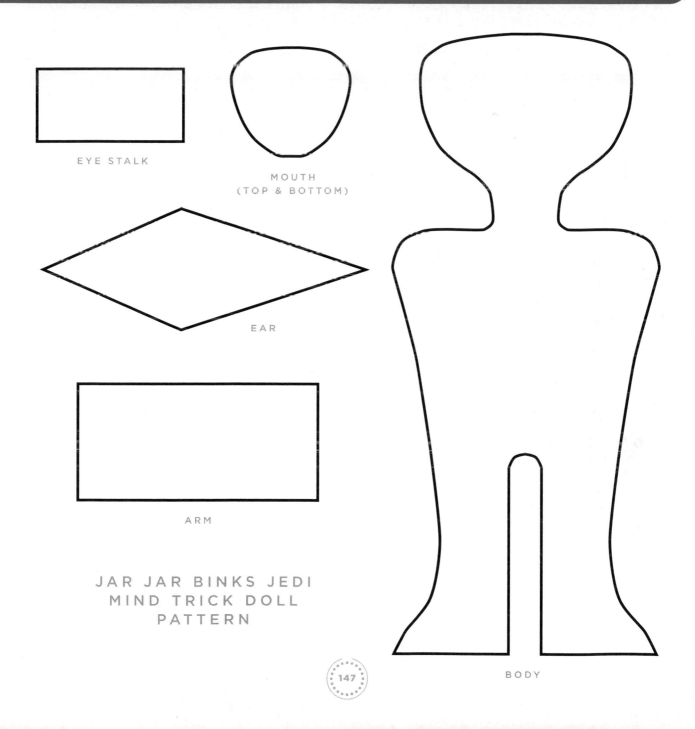

EYE STALK

MOUTH
(TOP & BOTTOM)

EAR

ARM

JAR JAR BINKS JEDI
MIND TRICK DOLL
PATTERN

147

BODY

BOSSK
BEAN
PORTRAIT

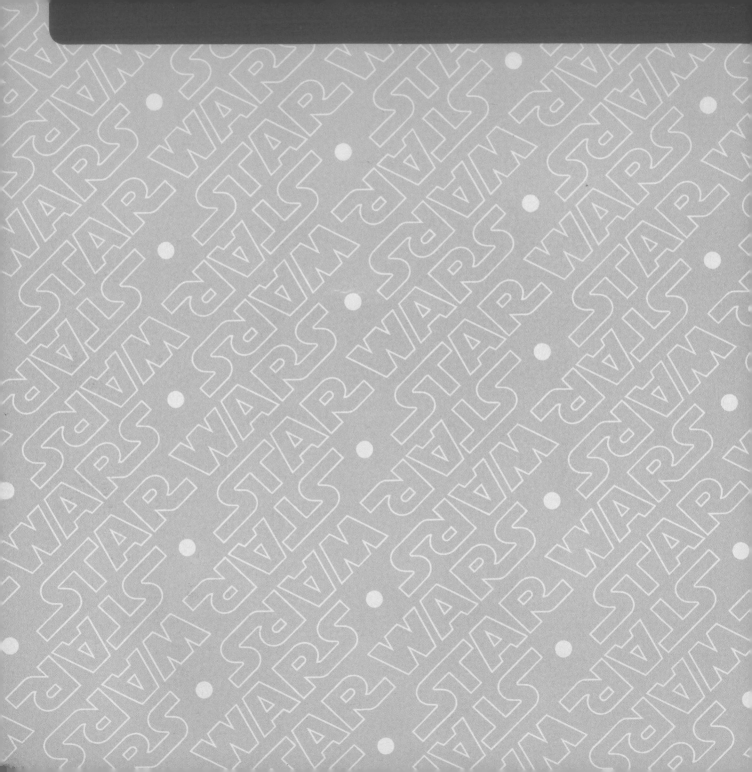

ABOUT THE AUTHOR

Author Bonnie Burton writes about Wookiees and Ewoks all day for Starwars.com while sewing Yoda felt dolls and mouse droid catnip toys at her desk at Lucasfilm. She's also written the books *You Can Draw: Star Wars* and *Draw Star Wars: The Clone Wars*, as well as the teen-girl advice book *Girls Against Girls*. When she's not in a galaxy far, far away, Bonnie turns old socks into monster puppets and blogs on her site Grrl.com.

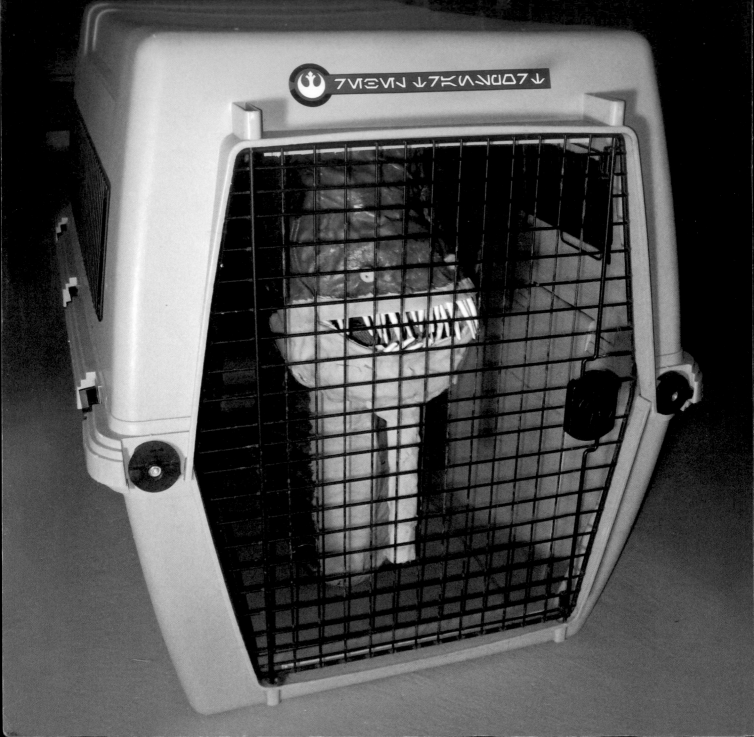

THE STAR WARS LIBRARY
TITAN BOOKS
OUT NOW

STAR WARS: THE COMPLETE STAR WARS ENCYCLOPEDIA

THE ART OF STAR WARS: THE CLONE WARS by Frank Parisi & Gary Scheppke

STAR WARS: THE FORCE UNLEASHED by Sean Williams

STAR WARS: THE ESSENTIAL ATLAS by Daniel Wallace & Jason Fry

STAR WARS: THE FORCE UNLEASHED II by Sean Williams

STAR WARS: THE OLD REPUBLIC: FATAL ALLIANCE by Sean Williams

STAR WARS: THE OLD REPUBLIC: DECEIVED by Paul S. Kemp

COMING SOON

STAR WARS: THE JEDI PATH: A MANUAL FOR STUDENTS OF THE FORCE by Daniel Wallace